Mrs. Traill

Afar in the Forest; or, Pictures of Life and Scenery in the Wilds of Canada

Mrs. Traill

Afar in the Forest; or, Pictures of Life and Scenery in the Wilds of Canada

ISBN/EAN: 9783337190729

Printed in Europe, USA, Canada, Australia, Japan

Cover: Foto ©Andreas Hilbeck / pixelio.de

More available books at **www.hansebooks.com**

AFAR IN THE FOREST;

OR,

PICTURES OF LIFE AND SCENERY

IN THE

WILDS OF CANADA.

By

MRS. TRAILL,
Author of "The Canadian Crusoes," &c.

LONDON:
T. NELSON AND SONS, PATERNOSTER ROW;
EDINBURGH; AND NEW YORK.

1869.

PREFACE

WE have much pleasure in placing before our readers a New and Revised Edition of a book which was formerly popular under the title of "LADY MARY AND HER NURSE." The present edition has been considerably improved, so as to increase its attractions for the young. It contains much pleasant information, and many interesting anecdotes respecting the plants and animals of our great Canadian Colony, and not a few lively details of the habits and customs of the Indians, now fast disappearing before the encroachments of European civilization. Both girl and boy may find amusement and instruction in these pages, whose perusal will advantageously occupy a leisure hour, and store their minds with many useful facts about the wild animals and natural curiosities of North America.

CHAPTER I.

The Flying Squirrel—Its Food—Story of a Wolf—Indian Village—Wild Rice.. 9

CHAPTER II.

Sleighing—Sleigh Robes—Fur Caps—Otter Skins—Old Snow-Storm—Otter Hunting—Otter Slides—Indian Names—Remarks on Wild Animals and their Habits.................... 26

CHAPTER III.

PART I.—Lady Mary reads to Mrs. Frazer the First Part of the History of the Squirrel Family............................ 36

PART II.—Which tells how the Gray Squirrels fared while they remained on Pine Island—How they behaved to their poor Relations, the Chitmunks—And what happened to them in the Forest 49

PART III.—How the Squirrels got to the Mill at the Rapids—And what happened to Velvet-paw 61

CHAPTER IV.

Squirrels—The Chitmunks—Docility of a Pet One—Roguery of a Yankee Pedlar—Return of the Musical Chitmunk to his Master's Bosom—Sagacity of a Black Squirrel............... 83

CHAPTER V.

Indian Baskets—Thread Plants—Maple Sugar-Tree—Indian Ornamental Works—Racoons................................ 95

CONTENTS.

CHAPTER VI.

Canadian Birds—Snow Sparrow—Robin Redbreast—Canadian Flowers—American Porcupine 108

CHAPTER VII.

Indian Bag—Indian Embroidery—Beaver's Tail—Beaver Architecture—Habits of the Beaver—Beaver Tools—Beaver Meadows... 119

CHAPTER VIII.

Indian Boy and his Pets—Tame Beaver at Home—Kitten, Wildfire—Pet Racoon and the Spaniel Puppies—Canadian Flora .. 132

CHAPTER IX.

Nurse tells Lady Mary about a Little Boy who was eaten by a Bear in the Province of New Brunswick—Of a Baby who was carried away, but taken alive—A Walk in the Garden—Humming-Birds—Canadian Balsams............................... 139

CHAPTER X.

Aurora Borealis, or Northern Lights, most frequently seen in northern Climates—Called Merry Dancers—Rose Tints—Tintlike Appearance—Lady Mary frightened 156

CHAPTER XI.

Strawberries—Canadian Wild Fruits—Wild Raspberries—The Hunter and the Lost Child—Cranberries—Cranberry Marshes—Nuts.. 163

CHAPTER XII.

Garter-snakes—Rattle-snakes—Anecdote of a Little Boy—Fisherman and Snake—Snake Charmers—Spiders—Land-Tortoise .. 178

CHAPTER XIII.

Ellen and her Pet Fawns—Docility of Fan—Jack's Droll Tricks—Affectionate Wolf—Fall Flowers—Departure of Lady Mary—The End.. 189

AFAR IN THE FOREST.

CHAPTER I.

THE FLYING SQUIRREL—ITS FOOD—STORY OF A WOLF—
INDIAN VILLAGE—WILD RICE.

"NURSE, what is the name of that pretty creature you have in your hand? What bright eyes it has! What a soft tail—just like a gray feather! Is it a little beaver?" asked the Governor's little daughter, as her nurse came into the room where her young charge, whom we shall call Lady Mary, was playing with her doll.

Carefully sheltered against her breast, its velvet nose just peeping from beneath her muslin neckerchief, the nurse held a small gray-furred animal, of the most delicate form and colour.

"No, my lady," she replied, "this is not a young beaver; a beaver is a much larger animal. A beaver's tail is not covered with fur; it is scaly, broad, and flat; it looks something like black leather,

10 AN EXCELLENT DISH.

THE FLYING SQUIRREL.

not very unlike that of my seal-skin slippers. The Indians eat beavers' tails at their great feasts, and think they make an excellent dish."

"If they are black, and look like leather shoes, I am very sure I should not like to eat them; so, if you please, Mrs. Frazer, do not let me have any beavers' tails cooked for my dinner," said the little lady, in a very decided tone.

"Indeed, my lady," replied her nurse, smiling, "it would not be an easy thing to obtain, if you wished to taste one, for beavers are not brought to our market. It is only the Indians and hunters who know how to trap them, and beavers are not so plentiful as they used to be."

Mrs. Frazer would have told Lady Mary a great deal about the way in which the trappers take the beavers, but the little girl interrupted her by saying, "Please, nurse, will you tell me the name of your pretty pet? Ah, sweet thing, what bright eyes you have!" she added, caressing the soft little head which was just seen from beneath the folds of the muslin handkerchief to which it timidly nestled, casting furtive glances at the admiring child, while the panting of its breast told the mortal terror that shook its frame whenever the little girl's hand was advanced to coax its soft back.

"It is a flying squirrel, Lady Mary," replied her nurse; "one of my brothers caught it a month ago, when he was chopping in the forest. He thought it might amuse your ladyship, and so he tamed it and sent it to me in a basket filled with moss, with some acorns, and hickory-nuts, and beech-mast for him to eat on his journey, for the little fellow has travelled a long way: he came from the beech-woods, near the town of Coburg, in the Upper Province."

"And where is Coburg, nurse? Is it a large city like Montreal or Quebec?"

"No, my lady; it is a large town on the shores of the great Lake Ontario."

"And are there many woods near it?"

"Yes; but not so many as there used to be many years ago. The forest is almost all cleared, and there are fields of wheat and Indian corn, and nice farms and pretty houses, where a few years back the lofty forest grew dark and thick."

"Nurse, you said there were acorns, and hickory-nuts, and beech-mast in the basket. I have seen acorns at home in dear England and Scotland, and I have eaten the hickory-nuts here; but what is beech-mast? Is it any part of a Canadian ship?"

The nurse smiled and said, "No, Lady Mary; it is the name that is given to the fruit of the beech-tree. You have seen the beech-tree in England; the nuts are enclosed in a rough and somewhat prickly husk, which opens when it is ripe at the top, and shows two or more three-cornered shining brown seeds, in a smooth, tough, leathery skin; these fall when the branches are shaken by the wind in autumn. Hogs fatten upon these nuts; and squirrels and dormice and wood-chucks gather them into their granaries for winter stores; and wild ducks and wild pigeons come from the far north at the season when the beech-mast fall to eat them; for God teaches these, his creatures, to know the times and the seasons when his bounteous hand is open to give them food from his boundless store. A great many other birds and beasts also feed upon the beech-mast."

"It was very good of your brother to send me this pretty creature, nurse," said the little lady; "I will ask papa to give him some money."

"There is no need of that, Lady Mary. My brother is not in want; he has a farm in the Upper Province, and is very well off."

"I am glad he is well off," said Lady Mary; "indeed, I do not see so many beggars here as in England."

"People need not beg in Canada, if they are well and strong and can work; a poor man can soon earn enough money to keep himself and his little ones."

"Nurse, will you be so kind as to ask Campbell to get a pretty cage for my squirrel? I will let him live close to my dormice, which will be pleasant company for my dear little squirrel, and I will feed him every day myself with nuts and sugar, and sweet cake and white bread. Now do not tremble and look so frightened, as though I were going to hurt you; and pray, Mr. Squirrel, do not bite. Oh! nurse, nurse, the wicked, spiteful creature has bitten my finger! See, see, it has made it bleed! Naughty thing! I will not love you if you bite. Pray, nurse, bind up my finger, or it will soil my frock."

Great was the pity bestowed upon the wound by Lady Mary's kind attendant, till the little girl, tired of hearing so much said about the bitten finger, gravely desired her maid to go in search of the cage and catch the truant, which had effected its escape, and was clinging to the curtains of the bed. The cage was procured—a large wooden cage, with an outer and an inner chamber, a bar for the little fellow to swing himself on, a drawer for his food, and a little dish for his water. The sleeping-room was furnished by the nurse with soft wool, and a fine store of nuts was put in the drawer; all his wants were well supplied, and Lady Mary watched the catching of the little animal with much interest. Great was the activity displayed by the runaway squirrel, and still greater the astonishment evinced by the Governor's little daughter at the flying leaps made by the squirrel in its attempts to elude the grasp of its pursuers.

"It flies! I am sure it must have wings. Look, look, nurse! it is here, now it is on the wall, now on the curtains! It must have wings; but it has no feathers!"

"It has no wings, dear lady, but it has a fine ridge of fur that covers a strong sinew or muscle between the fore and hinder legs; and it is by the help of this muscle that it is able to spring so far and so fast; and its claws are so sharp, that it can cling to a wall or any flat surface. The black and red squirrels, and the common gray, can jump very far and run up the bark of the trees very fast, but not so fast as the flying squirrel."

At last Lady Mary's maid, with the help of one of the housemaids, succeeded in catching the squirrel and securing him within his cage. But though Lady Mary tried all her words of endearment to coax the little creature to eat some of the good things that had been provided so liberally for his entertainment, he remained sullen and motionless at the bottom of the cage. A captive is no less a captive in a cage with gilded bars and with dainties to eat, than if rusted iron shut him in, and kept him from enjoying his freedom. It is for dear liberty that he pines and is sad, even in the midst of plenty!

"Dear nurse, why does my little squirrel tremble and look so unhappy? Tell me if he wants anything to eat that we have not given him. Why does he not lie down and sleep on the nice soft bed you have made for him in his little chamber? See, he has not tasted the nice sweet cake and sugar that I gave him."

"He is not used to such dainties, Lady Mary. In the forest he feeds upon hickory-nuts, and butter-nuts, and acorns, and beech-mast, and the buds of the spruce, fir and pine kernels, and many other seeds and nuts and berries that we could not get for him; he loves grain too, and Indian corn. He sleeps on green moss and leaves, and fine fibres of grass and roots, and drinks heaven's blessed dew, as it lies bright and pure upon the herbs of the field."

"Dear little squirrel! pretty creature! I know now what makes you sad. You long to be abroad among your own green woods, and sleeping on the soft green moss, which is far prettier than this ugly cotton wool. But you shall stay with me, my sweet one, till the cold winter is past and gone, and the spring flowers have come again; and then, my pretty squirrel, I will take you out of your dull cage, and we will go to St. Helen's green island, and I will let you go free; but I will put a scarlet collar about your neck before I let you go, that if any one finds you, they may know that you are my squirrel. Were you ever in the green forest, nurse? I hear papa talk about the 'Bush' and the 'Backwoods;' it must be very pleasant in the summer to live among the green trees. Were you ever there?"

"Yes, dear lady; I did live in the woods when I was a child. I was born in a little log-shanty, far, far away up the country, near a beautiful lake called Rice Lake, among woods, and valleys, and hills covered with flowers, and groves of pine, and white and black oaks."

"Stop, nurse, and tell me why they are called black and white; are the flowers black and white?"

"No, my lady; it is because the wood of the one is darker than the other, and the leaves of the black oak are dark and shining, while those of the white oak are brighter and lighter. The black oak is a beautiful tree. When I was a young girl, I used to like to climb the sides of the steep valleys, and look down upon the tops of the oaks that grew beneath, and to watch the wind lifting the boughs all glittering in the moonlight; they looked like a sea of ruffled green water. It is very solemn, Lady Mary, to be in the woods by night, and to hear no sound but the cry of the great wood-owl, or the voice of the whip-poor-will, calling to his fellow from the tamarack swamp, or, may be, the timid bleating of a fawn that has lost its mother, or the howl of a wolf."

"Nurse, I should be so afraid; I am sure I should cry if I heard the wicked wolves howling in the dark woods by night. Did you ever know any one who was eaten by a wolf?"

"No, my lady; the Canadian wolf is a great coward. I have heard the hunters say that they never attack any one unless there is a great flock together and the man is alone and unarmed. My uncle used to go out a great deal hunting, sometimes by torchlight, and sometimes on the lake, in a canoe with the Indians; and he shot and trapped a great many wolves and foxes and racoons. He has a great many heads of wild animals nailed up on the stoup in front of his log-house."

"Please tell me what a stoup is, nurse?"

"A verandah, my lady, is the same thing, only the old Dutch settlers gave it the name of a stoup, and the stoup is heavier and broader, and not quite so nicely made as a verandah. One day my uncle was crossing the lake on the ice; it was a cold winter afternoon; he was in a hurry to take some food to his brothers, who were drawing pine-logs in the

ADVENTURE WITH A WOLF.

bush. He had, besides a bag of meal and flour, a new axe on his shoulder. He heard steps as of a dog trotting after him; he turned his head, and there he saw, close at his heels, a big, hungry-looking gray wolf; he stopped and faced about, and the big beast stopped and showed his white sharp teeth. My uncle did not feel afraid, but looked steadily at the wolf, as much as to say, 'Follow me if you dare,' and walked on. When my uncle stopped, the wolf stopped; when he went on, the beast also went on."

"I would have run away," said Lady Mary.

"If my uncle had let the wolf see that he was afraid of him, he would have grown bolder, and have run after him and seized him. All animals are afraid of brave men, but not of cowards. When the beast came too near, my uncle faced him and showed the bright axe, and the wolf then shrank back a few paces. When my uncle got near the shore, he heard a long wild cry, as if from twenty wolves at once. It might have been the echoes from the islands that increased the sound; but it was very frightful and made his blood chill, for he knew that without his rifle he should stand a poor chance against a large pack of hungry wolves. Just then a gun went off; he heard the wolf give a terrible yell, he felt the whizzing of a bullet pass him, and turning about, saw the wolf lying dead on the ice. A loud shout from the cedars in front told him from whom the shot came; it was my father, who had been on the look-out on the lake shore, and he had fired at and hit the wolf when he saw that he could do so without hurting his brother."

"Nurse, it would have been a sad thing if the gun had shot your uncle."

"It would; but my father was one of the best shots in the district, and could hit a white spot on the bark of a tree with a precision that was perfectly wonderful. It was an old Indian from Buckhorn Lake who taught him to shoot deer by torchlight and to trap beavers."

"Well, I am glad that horrid wolf was killed, for wolves eat sheep and lambs; and I daresay they would devour my little squirrel if they could get him. Nurse, please to tell me again the name of the lake near which you were born."

"It is called Rice Lake, my lady. It is a fine piece of water, more than twenty miles long, and from three to five miles broad. It has pretty wooded islands, and several rivers or streams empty themselves into it. The Otonabee River is a fine broad stream, which flows through the forest a long way. Many years ago, there were no clearings on the banks, and no houses, only Indian tents or wigwams; but now there are a great many houses and farms."

"What are wigwams?"

"A sort of light tent, made with poles stuck into the ground in a circle, fastened together at the top, and covered on the outside with skins of wild animals, or with birch bark. The Indians light a fire of sticks and logs on the ground, in the middle of the wigwam, and lie or sit all round it; the smoke goes up to the top and escapes. Or sometimes, in the

INDIAN WIGWAMS.

warm summer weather, they kindle their fire without, and their squaws, or wives, attend to it; while they go hunting in the forest, or, mounted on swift horses, pursue the trail of their enemies. In the winter, they bank up the wigwam with snow, and make it very warm."

"I think it must be a very ugly sort of house, and I am glad I do not live in an Indian wigwam," said the little lady.

"The Indians are a very simple folk, my lady, and do not need fine houses like this in which your papa lives. They do not know the names or uses of half the fine things that are in the houses of the white people. They are happy and contented without them. It is not the richest that are happiest, Lady Mary, and the Lord careth for the poor and the lowly. There is a village on the shores of Rice Lake where the Indians live. It is not very pretty. The houses are all built of logs, and some of them have gardens and orchards. They have a neat church, and they have a good minister, who takes great pains to teach them the gospel of the Lord Jesus Christ. The poor Indians were Pagans until within the last few years."

"What are Pagans, nurse?"

"People, Lady Mary, who do not believe in God and the Lord Jesus Christ, our blessed Saviour."

"Nurse, is there real rice growing in the Rice Lake? I heard my governess say that rice grew only in warm countries. Now, your lake must be very cold if your uncle walked across the ice."

"This rice, my lady, is not real rice. I heard a gentleman tell my father that it was, properly speaking, a species of oats *—water oats, he called it; but the common name for it is wild rice. This wild rice grows in vast beds in the lake in patches of many acres. It will grow in water from eight to ten or twelve feet deep; the grassy leaves float upon the water like long narrow green ribbons. In the month of August, the stem that is to bear the flower and the grain rises straight up above the surface, and light delicate blossoms come out of a pale straw colour and lilac. They are very pretty, and wave

* Zizania, or water oats.

in the wind with a rustling noise. In the month of October, when the rice is ripe, the leaves turn yellow, and the rice-heads grow heavy and droop; then the squaws—as the Indian women are called—go out in their birch-bark canoes, holding in one hand a stick, in the other a short curved paddle with a sharp edge. With this they bend down the rice across the stick and strike off the heads, which fall into the canoe, as they push it along through the rice-beds. In this way they collect a great many bushels in the course of the day. The wild rice is not the least like the rice which your ladyship has eaten; it is thin, and covered with a light chaffy husk. The colour of the grain itself is a brownish-green, or olive, smooth, shining, and brittle. After separating the outward chaff, the squaws put by a large portion of the clean rice in its natural state for sale; for this they get from a dollar and a half to two dollars a bushel. Some they parch, either in large pots, or on mats made of the inner bark of cedar or bass wood, beneath which they light a slow fire, and plant around it a temporary hedge of green boughs closely set, to prevent the heat from escaping; they also drive stakes into the ground, over which they stretch the matting at a certain height above the fire. On this they spread the green rice, stirring it about with wooden paddles till it is properly parched; this is known by its bursting and showing the white grain of the flour. When quite cool it is stowed away in troughs, scooped out of butter-nut wood, or else sewed up in sheets of birch-bark or bass-mats, or in coarsely-made birch-bark baskets."

"And is the rice good to eat, nurse?"

"Some people like it as well as the white rice of Carolina; but it does not look so well. It is a great blessing to the poor Indians, who boil it in their soups, or eat it with maple molasses. And they eat it when parched without any other cooking, when they are on a long journey in the woods, or on the lakes. I have often eaten nice puddings made of it with milk. The deer feed upon the green rice. They swim into the water and eat the green leaves and tops. The Indians go out at night to shoot the deer on the water; they listen for them, and shoot them in the dark. The wild ducks and water-fowls come down in great flocks to fatten on the ripe rice in the fall of the year; also large flocks of rice buntings and red wings, which make their roosts among the low willows, flags, and lilies, close to the shallows of the lake."

"It seems very useful to birds as well as to men and beasts," said little Lady Mary.

"Yes, my lady, and to fishes also, I make no doubt; for the good God has cast it so abundantly abroad on the waters, that I daresay they also have their share. When the rice is fully ripe, the sun shining on it gives it a golden hue, just like a field of ripened grain. Surrounded by the deep-blue waters, it looks very pretty."

"I am very much obliged to you. nurse, for telling me so much about the Indian rice, and I will ask mamma to let me have some one day for my dinner, that I may know how it tastes."

Just then Lady Mary's governess came to bid her nurse dress her for a sleigh-ride, and so for the present we shall leave her; but we will tell our little readers something more in another chapter about Lady Mary and her flying squirrel.

CHAPTER II.

SLEIGHING—SLEIGH ROBES—FUR CAPS—OTTER SKINS—OLD SNOW-STORM—OTTER HUNTING—OTTER SLIDES—INDIAN NAMES—REMARKS ON WILD ANIMALS AND THEIR HABITS.

"NURSE, we have had a very nice sleigh-drive. I like sleighing very much over the white snow. The trees look so pretty, as if they were covered with white flowers, and the ground sparkled just like mamma's diamonds."

"It is pleasant, Lady Mary, to ride through the woods on a bright sunshiny day, after a fresh fall of snow. The young evergreens, hemlocks, balsams, and spruce-trees, are loaded with great masses of the new-fallen snow; while the slender saplings of the beech, birch, and basswood (the lime or linden) are bent down to the very ground, making bowers so bright and beautiful, you would be delighted to see them. Sometimes, as you drive along, great masses of the snow come showering down upon you; but it is so light and dry, that it shakes off without wetting you. It is pleasant to be wrapped up in warm blankets, or buffalo robes, at the bottom of a lumber-sleigh, and to travel through the forest by moonlight; the merry bells echoing through the silent woods, and the stars just peeping down through the frosted trees, which sparkle like diamonds in the moonbeams."

"Nurse, I should like to take a drive through the forest in winter. It is so nice to hear the sleigh-bells. We used sometimes to go out in the snow in Scotland, but we were in the carriage, and had no bells."

"No, Lady Mary; the snow seldom lies long enough in the old country to make it worth while to have sleighs there; but in Russia and Sweden, and other cold Northern countries, they use sleighs with bells."

Lady Mary ran to the little bookcase where she had a collection of children's books, and very soon found a picture of Laplanders and Russians wrapped in furs.

"How long will the winter last, nurse?" said the child, after she had tired herself with looking at the prints; "a long, long time—a great many weeks?—a great many months?"

"Yes, my lady; five or six months."

"Oh, that is nice—nearly half a year of white snow, and sleigh-drives every day, and bells ringing all the time! I tried to make out a tune, but they only seemed to say, 'Up-hill, up-hill! down-hill, down-hill!' all the way. Nurse, please tell me what are sleigh-robes made of?"

"Some sleigh-robes, Lady Mary, are made of bear-skins, lined with red or blue flannel; some are of wolf-skins, lined with bright scarlet cloth; and some of racoon; the commonest are buffalo-skins; I have seen some of deer-skins, but these last are not so good, as the hair comes off, and they are not so warm as the skins of the furred or woolly-coated animals."

"I sometimes see long tails hanging down over the backs of the sleigh and cutters—they look very pretty, like the end of mamma's boa."

"The wolf and racoon skin robes are generally made up with the tails, and sometimes the heads of the animals are also left. I noticed the head of a wolf, with its sharp ears, and long white teeth, looking very fierce, at the back of a cutter, the other day."

"Nurse, that must have looked very droll. Do you know I saw a gentleman the other day, walking with papa, who had a fox-skin cap on his head, and the fox's nose was just peeping over his shoulder, and the tail hung down his back, and I saw its bright black eyes looking so cunning. I thought it must be alive, and that it had curled itself round his head; but the gentleman took it off, and showed me that the eyes were glass."

"Some hunters, Lady Mary, make caps of otter, mink, or badger skins, and ornament them with the tails, heads, and claws."

"I have seen a picture of the otter, nurse; it is a pretty, soft-looking thing, with a round head and black eyes. Where do otters live?"

"The Canadian otters, Lady Mary, live in holes in the banks of sedgy, shallow lakes, mill-ponds, and sheltered creeks. The Indian hunters find their haunts by tracking their steps in the snow; for an Indian or Canadian hunter knows the track made by any bird or beast, from the deep broad print of the bear, to the tiny one of the little shrewmouse, which is the smallest four-footed beast in this or any other country.

"Indians catch the otter, and many other wild animals, in a sort of trap, which they call a 'deadfall.' Wolves are often so trapped, and then shot. The Indians catch the otter for the sake of its dark shining fur, which is used by the hatters and furriers. Old Jacob Snow-storm, an old Indian who lived on the banks of the Rice Lake, used to catch otters; and I have often listened to him, and laughed at his stories."

"Do, please, nurse, tell me what old Jacob Snow-storm told you about the otters; I like to hear stories about wild beasts. But what a droll surname Snow-storm is!"

"Yes, Lady Mary; Indians have very odd names; they are called after all sorts of strange things. They do not name the children, as we do, soon after they are born, but wait for some remarkable circumstance, some dream or accident. Some call them after the first strange animal or bird that appears to the new-born. Old Snow-storm most likely owed his name to a heavy fall of snow when he was a baby. I knew a chief named Musk-rat, and a pretty Indian girl who was named 'Badau'-bun '— *Light of the Morning.*"

"And what is the Indian name for Old Snow-storm?"

"'Be-che-go-ke-poor,' my lady."

Lady Mary said it was a funny sounding name, and not at all like Snow-storm, which she liked a great deal better; and she was much amused while her nurse repeated to her some names of squaws and papooses (Indian women and children); such as Long Thrush, Little Fox, Running Stream, Snow-bird, Red Cloud, Young Eagle, Big Bush, and many others.

"Now, nurse, will you tell me some more about Jacob Snow-storm and the otters?"

"Well, Lady Mary, the old man had a cap of otter-skin, of which he was very proud, and only wore on great days. One day as he was playing with it, he said:—' Otter funny fellow; he like play too, sometimes. Indian go hunting up Ottawa, that great big river, you know. Go one moonlight night; lie down under bushes in snow; see lot of little fellow and big fellow at play. Run up and down bank; bank all ice. Sit down top of bank; good slide there. Down he go splash into water; out again. Funny fellow those!' And then the old hunter threw back his head, and laughed, till you could have seen all his white teeth, he opened his mouth so wide."

THE OTTERS.

Lady Mary was very much amused at the comical way in which the old Indian talked.

"Can otters swim, nurse?"

"Yes, Lady Mary; the good God who has created all things well, has given to this animal webbed feet, which enable it to swim; and it can also dive down in the deep water, where it finds fish and mussels, and perhaps the roots of some water-plants to eat. It makes very little motion or disturbance in the water when it goes down in search of its prey. Its coat is thick, and formed of two kinds of hair; the outer hair is long, silky, and shining; the under part is short, fine, and warm. The water cannot penetrate to wet them,—the oily nature of the fur throws off the moisture. They dig large holes with their claws, which are short, but very strong. They line their nests with dry grass, and rushes, and roots gnawed fine, and do not pass the winter in sleep, as the dormice, flying squirrels, racoons, and bears do. They are very innocent and playful, both when young, and even after they grow old. The lumberers often tame them, and they become so docile that they will come at a call or whistle. Like all wild animals, they are most lively at night, when they come out to feed and play."

"Dear little things! I should like to have a tame otter to play with, and run after me; but do you think he would eat my squirrel? You know cats will eat squirrels—so mamma says."

"Cats belong to a very different class of animals; they are beasts of prey, formed to spring and bound, and tear with their teeth and claws. The otter is also a beast of prey, but its prey is found in the still waters, and not on the land; it can neither climb nor leap. So I do not think he would hurt your squirrel, if you had one."

"See, nurse, my dear little squirrel is still where I left him, clinging to the wires of the cage, his bright eyes looking like two black beads.'

"As soon as it grows dark he will begin to be more lively, and perhaps he will eat something, but not while we look at him—he is too shy for that."

"Nurse, how can they see to eat in the dark?"

"The good God, Lady Mary, has so formed their eyes that they can see best by night. I will read you, Lady Mary, a few verses from Psalm civ. :—

"'Verse 19. He appointed the moon for seasons: the sun knoweth his going down.

"'20. Thou makest darkness, and it is night: wherein all the beasts of the forest do creep forth.

"'21. The young lions roar after their prey, and seek their meat from God.

"'22. The sun ariseth, they gather themselves together, and lay them down in their dens.

"'23. Man goeth forth unto his work and to his labour, until the evening.

"'24. O Lord, how manifold are thy works! in wisdom hast thou made them all: the earth is full of thy riches.'

"Thus you see, my dear lady, that our heavenly Father taketh care of all his creatures, and provideth for them both by day and by night."

"I remember, nurse, that my dormice used to lie quite still, nestled among the moss and wool in their little dark chamber in the cage, all day long; but when it was night they used to come out and frisk about, and run along the wires, and play all sorts of tricks, chasing one another round and round, and they were not afraid of me, but would let me look at them while they ate a nut, or a bit of sugar; and

HOW THE DORMICE FEED.

LADY MARY SLEIGHING HER DOLL.

the dear little things would drink out of their little white saucer, and wash their faces and tails—it was so pretty to see them!"

"Did you notice, Lady Mary, how the dormice held their food?"

"Yes; they sat up, and held it in their fore-paws, which looked just like tiny hands."

"There are many animals whose fore-feet resemble hands, and these, generally, convey their food to their mouths—among these are the squirrel and dormice. They are good climbers and diggers. You see, my dear young lady, how the merciful Creator has given to all his creatures, however lowly, the best means of supplying their wants, whether of food or shelter."

"Indeed, nurse, I have learned a great deal about squirrels, Canadian rice, otters, and Indians; but, if you please, I must now have a little play with my doll. Good-bye, Mrs. Frazer; pray take care of my dear little squirrel, and mind that he does not fly away." And Lady Mary was soon busily engaged in drawing her wax doll about the nursery in a little sleigh lined with red squirrel fur robes, and talking to her as all children like to talk to their dolls, whether they be rich or poor—the children of peasants, or governors' daughters.

CHAPTER III.

LADY MARY READS TO MRS. FRAZER THE FIRST PART OF THE HISTORY OF THE SQUIRREL FAMILY.

ONE day Lady Mary came to her nurse, and putting her arms about her neck, whispered to her,—"Mrs. Frazer, my dear good governess has given me something—it is in my hand," and she slily held her hand behind her—"will you guess what it is?"

"Is it a book, my lady?"

"Yes, yes, it is a book, a pretty book; and see, here are pictures of squirrels in it. Mrs. Frazer, if you like, I will sit down on this cushion by you and read some of my new book. It does not seem very hard."

Then Mrs. Frazer took out her work-basket and sat down to sew, and Lady Mary began to read the little story, which, I hope, may entertain my little readers as much as it did the Governor's daughter.

Part I.

THE HISTORY OF A SQUIRREL FAMILY.

It must be a pleasant thing to be a squirrel, and live a life of freedom in the boundless forests; to leap and bound among the branches of the tall trees; to gambol in the deep shade of the cool glossy leaves, through the long warm summer day; to gather the fresh nuts and berries; to drink the pure dews of heaven, all bright and sparkling

LADY MARY READING HER PICTURE-BOOK.

from the opening flowers; to sleep on soft beds of moss and thistle-down in some hollow branch rocked by the wind as in a cradle. Yet, though this was the happy life led by a family of pretty gray squirrels that had their dwelling in the hoary branch of an old oak-tree that grew on one of the rocky islands in a beautiful lake in Upper Canada, called *Stony Lake* (because it was full of rocky islands), these little creatures were far from being contented, and were always wishing for a change. Indeed, they had been very happy, till one day when a great black squirrel swam to the island and paid them a visit. He was a very fine handsome fellow, nearly twice as large as any of the gray squirrels; he had a tail that flourished over his back, when he set it up, like a great black feather; his claws were sharp and strong, and his eyes very round and bright; he had upright ears, and long, sharp teeth, of which he made good use. The old gray squirrels called him cousin, and invited him to dinner. They very civilly set before him some acorns and beech-nuts; but he proved a hungry visitor, and ate as much as would have fed the whole family for a week. After the gray squirrels had cleared away the shells and scraps, they asked their greedy guest where he came from, when Blackie told them he was a great traveller, and had seen many wonderful things; that he had once lived on a forked pine at the head of the Waterfall, but being tired of a dull life, he had gone out on his travels to see the world; that he had been down the lake, and along the river shore, where there were great places cut out in the thick forest, called clearings, where some very tall creatures lived, who were called men and women, with young ones called children; that though they were not so pretty as squirrels—for they had no fur on them, and were obliged to make clothes to cover them and keep them warm—they were very useful, and sowed corn and planted fruit-trees and roots for squirrels to eat, and even built large grain stores to keep it safe and dry for them.

This seemed very strange, and the simple little gray squirrels were very much pleased, and said they should like very much to go down the lakes too, and see these wonderful things.

The black squirrel then told them that there were many things to be seen in these clearings; that there were large beasts, called oxen, and cows, and sheep, and pigs; and these creatures had houses built for them to live in; and all the men and women seemed to employ themselves about, was feeding and taking care of them.

Now this cunning fellow never told his simple cousins that the oxen had to bear a heavy wooden yoke and chain, and were made to work very hard; nor that the cows were fed that they might give milk to the children; nor that the pigs were fatted to make pork; nor that the sheep had their warm fleeces cut off every year that the settlers might have the wool to spin and weave. Blackie did not say that the men carried guns, and the dogs were fierce, and would hunt poor squirrels from tree to tree, frightening them almost to death with their loud, angry barking; that cats haunted the barns and houses; and, in short, that there were dangers as well as pleasures to be met with in these clearings; and that the barns were built to shelter the grain for men, and not for the benefit of squirrels.

The black squirrel proved rather a troublesome guest, for he stayed several days, and ate so heartily, that the old gray squirrels were obliged to hint that he had better go back to the clearings, where there was so much food, for that their store was nearly done.

When Blackie found that all the nice nuts were eaten, and that even pine-kernels and beech-nuts were becoming scarce, he went away, saying that he should soon come again.

The old gray squirrels were glad when they saw the tip of Blackie's tail disappear, as he whisked down the trunk of the old oak; but their young ones were very sorry that he was gone, for they liked very much to listen to all his wonderful stories, which they thought were true; and they told their father and mother how they wished they would leave the dull island and the old tree, and go down the lakes, and see the wonderful things that their black cousin had described.

But the old ones shook their heads, and said they feared there was more fiction than truth in the tales they had heard, and that if they were wise they would stay where they were. "What do you want more, my dear children," said their mother, "than you enjoy here? Have you not this grand old oak for a palace to live in; its leaves and branches spreading like a canopy over your heads, to shelter you from the hot sun by day and the dews by night? Are there not moss, dried grass, and roots beneath, to make a soft bed for you to lie upon? and do not the boughs drop down a plentiful store of brown ripe acorns? That silver lake, studded with islands of all shapes and sizes, produces cool clear water for you to drink and bathe yourselves in. Look at those flowers that droop their blossoms down to its glassy surface, and the white lilies that rest upon its bosom,—will you see anything fairer or better if you leave this place? Stay at home and be contented."

"If I hear any more grumbling," said their father, "I shall pinch your ears and tails." So the little squirrels said no more, but I am sorry to say they did not pay much heed to their wise old mother's counsels; for whenever they were alone, all their talk was how to run away, and go abroad to see the world, as their black cousin had called the new settlement down the lakes. It never came into the heads of the silly creatures that those wonderful stories they had been told originated in an artful scheme of the greedy black squirrel, to induce them to leave their warm pleasant house in the oak, that he and his children might come and live in it, and get the hoards of grain, and nuts, and acorns, that their father and mother had been laying up for winter stores.

Moreover, the wily black squirrel had privately told them that their father and mother intended to turn them out of the nest very soon, and make provision for a new family. This indeed was really the case; for as soon as young animals can provide for themselves, their parents turn them off, and care no more for them. Very different, indeed, is this from our parents; for they love and cherish us as long as they live, and afford us a home and shelter as long as we need it.

Every hour these little gray squirrels grew more and more impatient to leave the lonely little rocky island, though it was a pretty spot, and the place of their birth; but they were now eager to go abroad and seek their fortunes.

"Let us keep our own counsel," said Nimble-foot to his sisters Velvet-paw and Silver-nose, " or we may chance to get our tails pulled; but be all ready for a start by early dawn to-morrow."

Velvet-paw and Silver-nose said they would be up before sunrise, as they should have a long voyage down the lake, and agreed to rest on Pine Island near the opening of Clear Lake. " And then take to the shore and travel through the woods, where, no doubt, we shall have a pleasant time," said Nimble-foot, who was the most hopeful of the party.

The sun was scarcely yet risen over the fringe of dark pines that skirted the shores of the lake, and a soft creamy mist hung on the surface of the still waters, which were unruffled by the slightest breeze. The little gray squirrels awoke, and looked sleepily out from the leafy screen that shaded their mossy nest. The early notes of the wood-thrush and song-sparrow, with the tender warbling of the tiny wren, sounded sweetly in the still, dewy morning air; while from a cedar swamp was heard the trill of the green frogs, which the squirrels thought very pretty music. As the sun rose above the tops of the trees, the mist rolled off in light fleecy clouds, and soon was lost in the blue sky, or lay in large bright drops on the cool grass and shining leaves. Then all the birds awoke, and the insects shook their gauzy wings which had been folded all the night in the flower-cups, and the flowers began to lift their heads, and the leaves to expand to catch the golden light. There was a murmur on the water as it played among the sedges, and lifted the broad floating leaves of the white water-lilies, with their carved ivory cups; and the great green, brown, and blue dragon-flies rose with a whirring sound, and darted to and fro among the water-flowers.

It is a glorious sight to see the sun rise at any time, for then we can look upon him without having our eyes dazzled with the brightness of his beams; and though there were no men and women and little children, in the lonely waters and woods, to lift up their hands and voices in prayer and praise to God, who makes the sun to rise each day, yet no doubt the great Creator is pleased to see his creatures rejoice in the blessings of light and heat.

Lightly running down the rugged bark of the old

oak-tree, the little squirrels bade farewell to their island home—to the rocks, mosses, ferns, and flowers that had sheltered them, among which they had so often chased each other in merry gambols. They thought little of all this, when they launched themselves on the silver bosom of the cool lake.

"How easy it is to swim in this clear water!" said Silver-nose to her sister Velvet-paw. "We shall not be long in reaching yonder island, and there, no doubt, we shall get a good breakfast."

So the little swimmers proceeded on their voyage, furrowing the calm waters as they glided noiselessly along; their soft gray heads and ears and round black eyes only being seen, and the bright streaks caused by the motion of their tails, which lay flat on the surface, looking like silver threads gently floating on the stream.

Not being much used to the fatigue of swimming, the little squirrels were soon tired, and if it had not been for a friendly bit of stick that happened to float near her, poor Velvet-paw would have been drowned; however, she got up on the stick, and, setting up her fine broad tail, went merrily on, and soon passed Nimble-foot and Silver-nose. The current drew the stick towards the Pine Island that lay at the entrance of Clear Lake, and Velvet-paw leaped ashore, and sat down on a mossy stone to dry her fur, and watch for her brother and sister: they, too, found a large piece of birch-bark which the winds had blown into the water, and as a little breeze had sprung up to waft them along, they were not very long before they landed on the island. They were all very glad when they met again, after the perils and fatigues of the voyage. The first thing to be done was to look for something to eat, for their early rising had made them very hungry. They found abundance of pine-cones strewn on the ground, but, alas for our little squirrels! very few kernels in them; for the crossbills and chiccadees had been at work for many weeks on the trees; and also many families of their poor relations, the chitmunks or ground squirrels, had not been idle, as our little voyagers could easily guess by the chips and empty cones round their holes. So, weary as they were, they were obliged to run up the tall pine and hemlock trees, to search among the cones that grew on their very top branches. While our squirrels were busy with the few kernels they chanced to find, they were started from their repast by the screams of a large slate-coloured hawk, and Velvet-paw very narrowly escaped being pounced upon and carried off in its sharp-hooked talons. Silver-nose at the same time was nearly frightened to death by the keen round eyes of a cunning racoon, which had come within a few feet of the mossy branch of an old cedar, where she sat picking the seeds out of a dry head of a blue flag-flower she had found on the shore. Silvy, at this sight, gave a spring that left her many yards beyond her sharp-sighted enemy.

A lively note of joy was uttered by Nimble-foot,

for, perched at his ease on a top branch of the hemlock-tree, he had seen the bound made by Silver-nose.

"Well jumped, Silvy," said he; "Mister Coon must be a smart fellow to equal that. But look sharp, or you will get your neck wrung yet; I see we must keep a good look-out in this strange country."

"I begin to wish we were safe back again in our old one," whined Silvy, who was much frightened by the danger she had just escaped.

"Pooh, pooh, child; don't be a coward," said Nimble, laughing.

"Cousin Blackie never told us there were hawks and coons on this island," said Velvet-paw.

"My dear, he thought we were too brave to be afraid of hawks and coons," said Nimble. "For my part, I think it is a fine thing to go out a little into the world. We should never see anything better than the sky, and the water, and the old oak-tree on that little island."

"Ay, but I think it is safer to see than to be seen," said Silvy, "for hawks and eagles have strong beaks, and racoons sharp claws and hungry-looking teeth; and it is not very pleasant, Nimble, to be obliged to look out for such wicked creatures."

"Oh, true indeed," said Nimble; "if it had not been for that famous jump you made, Silvy, and, Velvet, your two admirers, the hawk and racoon, would soon have hid all your beauties from the world, and put a stop to your travels."

"It is very well for brother Nimble to make light of our dangers," whispered Velvet-paw, " but let us see how he will jump if a big eagle were to pounce down to carry him off."

"Yes, yes," said Silvy; "it is easy to brag before one is in danger."

The squirrels thought they would now go and look for some partridge-berries, of which they were very fond, for the pine-kernels were but dry husky food after all.

There were plenty of the pretty white star-shaped blossoms, growing all over the ground under the pine-trees, but the bright scarlet twin-berries were not yet ripe. In winter the partridges eat this fruit from under the snow; and it furnishes food for many little animals as well as birds. The leaves are small, of a dark green, and the white flowers have a very fine fragrant scent. Though the runaways found none of these berries fit to eat, they saw some ripe strawberries among the bushes; and, having satisfied their hunger, began to grow very merry, and whisked here and there and everywhere, peeping into this hole and under that stone. Sometimes they had a good game of play, chasing one another up and down the trees, chattering and squeaking as gray squirrels only can chatter and squeak, when they are gambolling about in the wild woods of Canada.

Indeed, they made such a noise, that the great ugly black snakes lifted up their heads, and stared at them with their wicked spiteful-looking eyes, and the little ducklings swimming among the water-lilies gathered round their mother, and a red-winged blackbird perched on a dead tree gave alarm to the rest of the flock by calling out, *Geck, geck, geck,* as loudly as he could. In the midst of their frolics, Nimble skipped into a hollow log—but was glad to run out again; for a porcupine covered with sharp spines was there, and was so angry at being disturbed, that he stuck one of his spines into poor Nimble-foot's soft velvet nose, and there it would have remained if Silvy had not seized it with her teeth and pulled it out. Nimble-foot squeaked sadly, and would not play any longer, but rolled himself up and went to sleep in a red-headed woodpecker's old nest; while Silvy and Velvet-paw frisked about in the moonlight, and when tired of play got up into an old oak which had a large hollow place in the crown of it, and fell asleep, fancying, no doubt, that they were on the rocky island in Stony Lake; and so we will bid them good night, and wish them pleasant dreams.

Lady Mary had read a long while, and was now tired; so she kissed her nurse, and said, "Now, Mrs. Frazer, I will play with my doll, and feed my squirrel and my dormice."

The dormice were two soft, brown creatures, almost as pretty and as innocent as the squirrel, and a great deal tamer; and they were called Jeannette and Jeannot, and would come when they were called by their names, and take a bit of cake or a lump of sugar out of the fingers of their little mistress. Lady Mary had two canaries, Dick and Pet; and she loved her dormice and birds, and her new pet, the flying squirrel, very much, and never let them want for food, or water, or any nice thing she could get for them. She liked the history of the gray squirrels very much; and was quite eager to get her book the next afternoon, to read the second part of the adventures and wanderings of the family.

Part II.

WHICH TELLS HOW THE GRAY SQUIRRELS GET ON WHILE THEY REMAINED ON PINE ISLAND—HOW THEY BEHAVED TO THEIR POOR RELATIONS, THE CHITMUNKS—AND WHAT HAPPENED TO THEM IN THE FOREST.

It was noon when the little squirrels awoke, and, of course, they were quite ready for their breakfast; but there was no good, kind old mother to provide for their wants, and to bring nuts, acorns, roots, or fruit for them; they must now get up, go forth, and seek food for themselves. When Velvet-paw and Silver-nose went to call Nimble-foot, they were surprised to find his nest empty; but after searching a long while, they found him sitting on the root of an up-turned tree, looking at a family of little chit-

UNCOURTEOUS BEHAVIOUR.

THE GRAY SQUIRREL AND THE CHITMUNKS.

munks busily picking over the pine-cones on the ground; but as soon as one of the poor little fellows, with great labour, had dug out a kernel, and was preparing to eat it, down leaped Nimble-foot and carried off the prize; and if one of the little chitmunks ventured to say a word, he very uncivilly gave him a scratch, or bit his ears, calling him a mean, shabby fellow.

Now the chitmunks were really very pretty. They were, to be sure, not more than half the size of the gray squirrels, and their fur was short, without the soft, thick glossy look upon it of the gray squirrels'. They were of a lively, tawny yellow-brown colour, with long black and white stripes down their backs; their tails were not so long nor so thickly furred; and instead of living in the trees, they made their nests in logs and windfalls, and had their granaries and winter houses too underground, where they made warm nests of dried moss and grass and thistledown; to these they had several entrances, so that they had always a chance of refuge if danger were nigh. Like the dormice, flying squirrels, and ground hogs, they slept soundly during the cold weather, only awakening when the warm spring sun had melted the snow.*

The vain little gray squirrels thought themselves much better than these little chitmunks, whom they treated with very little politeness, laughing at them for living in holes in the ground, instead of upon lofty trees, as they did; they even called them low-

* It is not quite certain that the chitmunk is a true squirrel, and he is sometimes called a striped rat. This pretty animal seems, indeed, to form a link between the rat and squirrel.

bred fellows, and wondered why they did not imitate their high-breeding and behaviour.

The chitmunks took very little notice of their rudeness, but merely said that, if being high-bred made people rude, they would rather remain humble as they were.

"As we are the head of all the squirrel families," said Silver-nose, "we shall do you the honour of breakfasting with you to-day."

"We breakfasted hours ago, while you lazy fellows were fast asleep," replied an old chitmunk, poking his little nose out of a hole in the ground.

"Then we shall dine with you; so make haste and get something good for us," said Nimble-foot. "I have no doubt you have plenty of butter and hickory-nuts laid up in your holes."

The old chitmunk told him he might come and get them, if he could.

At this the gray squirrels skipped down from the branches, and began to run hither and thither, and to scratch among the moss and leaves, to find the entrance to the chitmunks' grain stores. They peeped under the old twisted roots of the pines and cedars, into every chink and cranny, but no sign of a granary was to be seen.

Then the chitmunks said, "My dear friends, this is a bad season to visit us; we are very poor just now, finding it difficult to get a few dry pine-kernels and berries; but if you will come and see us after harvest, we shall have a store of nuts and acorns."

"Pretty fellows you are!" replied Nimble, "to put us off with promises, when we are so hungry; we might starve between this and harvest."

"If you leave this island, and go down the lake, you will come to a mill, where the red squirrels live, and where you will have fine times," said one of the chitmunks.

"Which is the nearest way to the mill?" asked Velvet-paw.

"Swim to the shore, and keep the Indian path, and you will soon see it."

But while the gray squirrels were looking out for the path, the cunning chitmunks whisked away into their holes, and left the inquirers in the lurch, who could not tell what had become of them; for though they did find a round hole that they thought might be one of their burrows, it was so narrow that they could only poke in their noses, but could get no further—the gray squirrels being much fatter and bigger than the slim little chitmunks.

"After all," said Silvy, who was the best of the three, "perhaps, if we had been civil, the chitmunks would have treated us better."

"Well," said Nimble, "if they had been good fellows, they would have invited us, as our mother did Cousin Blackie, and have set before us the best they had. I could find it in my heart to dig them out of their holes and give them a good bite." This was all brag on Nimble's part, who was not near so brave as he wished Silvy and Velvet-paw to suppose he was.

After spending some time in hunting for acorns, they made up their minds to leave the island, and as it was not very far to the mainland, they decided on swimming thither.

"Indeed," said Silver-nose, "I am tired of this dull place; we are not better off here than we were in the little island in Stony Lake, where our good old mother took care we should have plenty to eat, and we had a nice warm nest to shelter us."

"Ah, well, it is of no use grumbling now; if we were to go back, we should only get a scolding, and perhaps be chased off the island," said Nimble. "Now let us have a race, and see which of us will get to shore first;" and he leaped over Velvet-paw's head, and was soon swimming merrily for the shore. He was soon followed by his companions, and in half an hour they were all safely landed. Instead of going into the thick forest, they agreed to take the path by the margin of the lake, for there they had a better chance of getting nuts and fruit; but though it was the merry month of June, and there were plenty of pretty flowers in bloom, the berries were hardly ripe, and our little vagrants fared but badly. Besides being hungry, they were sadly afraid of the eagles and fish-hawks that kept hovering over the water; and when they went further into the forest to avoid them, they saw a great white wood-owl, noiselessly flying out from among the close cedar swamps, that seemed just ready to pounce down upon them. The gray squirrels did not like the look of the owl's great round shining eyes, as they peered at them, under the tufts of silky white feathers, which almost hid his hooked bill, and their hearts sunk within them when they heard his hollow cry, "*Ho, ho, ho, ho!*" "*Waugh, ho!*" dismally sounding in their ears.

It was well that Velvet-paw was as swift afoot as she was soft, for one of these great owls had very nearly caught her, while she was eating a filbert that she had found in a cleft branch, where a nuthatch had fixed it, while she pecked a hole in the shell. Some bird of prey had scared away the poor nuthatch, and Velvet-paw no doubt thought she was in luck when she found the prize; but it would have been a dear nut to her, if Nimble, who was a sharp-sighted fellow, had not seen the owl, and cried, "*Chit, chit, chit, chit!*" to warn her of her danger. "*Chit, chit, chit, chit!*" cried Velvet-paw, and away she flew to the very top of a tall pine-tree, springing from one tree-top to another, till she was soon out of the old owl's reach.

"What shall we do for supper to-night?" said Silver-nose, looking very pitifully at Nimble-foot, whom they looked upon as the head of the family.

"We shall not want for a good supper and breakfast too, or I am very much mistaken. Do you see that red squirrel yonder, climbing the hemlock-tree? Well, my dears, he has a fine store of good things in that beech-tree. I watched him run down with a nut in his teeth. Let us wait patiently, and we shall see him come again for another; and as soon as he has done his meal, we will go and take ours."

The red squirrel ran to and fro several times, each time carrying off a nut to his nest in the hemlock; after a while, he came no more. As soon as he was out of sight, Nimble led the way and found the hoard. The beech was quite hollow in the heart; and they went down through a hole in the branch, and found a store of hazel-nuts, with acorns, hickory-nuts, butter-nuts, and beech-mast, all packed quite close and dry. They soon made a great hole in the red squirrel's store of provisions, and were just choosing some nuts to carry off with them, when they were disturbed by a scratching against the bark of the tree. Nimble, who was always the first to take care of himself, gave the alarm, and he and Velvet-paw, being nearest to the hole, got off safely; but poor Silvy had the ill luck to sneeze, and before she had time to hide herself, the angry red squirrel sprang upon her, and gave her such a terrible cuffing and scratching, that Silvy cried out for mercy. As to Nimble-foot and Velvet-paw, they paid no heed to her cries for help; they ran away, and left her to bear the blame of all their misdeeds as well as her own. Thieves are always cowards, and are sure to forsake one another when danger is nigh.

The angry red squirrel pushed poor Silvy out of her granary, and she was glad to crawl away and hide herself in a hole at the root of a neighbouring tree, where she lay in great pain and terror, licking her wounds and crying to think how cruel it was of her brother and sister to leave her to the mercy of the red squirrel. It was surely very cowardly of Nimble-foot and Velvet-paw to forsake her in such a time of need; nor was this the only danger that befell poor Silvy. One morning, when she put her nose out of the hole to look about her before venturing out, she saw seated on a branch, close beside the tree she was under, a racoon, staring full at her with his sharp cunning black eyes. She was very much afraid of him, for she thought he looked very hungry; but as she knew that racoons are very fond of nuts and fruit, she said to herself, "Perhaps if I show him where the red squirrel's granary in the beech-tree is, he will not kill me." Then she said very softly to him, "Good Mister Coon, if you want a very nice breakfast, and will promise to do me no hurt, I will tell you where to find plenty of nuts."

The coon eyed her with a sly grin, and said, "If I can get anything more to my taste than a pretty gray squirrel, I will take it, my dear, and not lay a paw upon your soft back."

"Ah, but you must promise not to touch me, if I come out and show you where to find the nuts," said Silvy.

"Upon the word and honour of a coon!" replied the racoon, laying one black paw upon his breast; "but if you do not come out of your hole, I shall soon come and dig you out, so you had best be quick; and if you trust me, you shall come to no hurt."

Then Silvy thought it wisest to seem to trust the racoon's word, and she came out of her hole, and went a few paces to point out the tree where her enemy the red squirrel's store of nuts was; but as soon as she saw Mister Coon disappear in the hollow of the tree, she bade him good-bye, and whisked up a tall tree, where she knew the racoon could not reach her; and having now quite recovered her strength, she was able to leap from branch to branch, and even from one tree to another, whenever they grew close and the boughs touched, as they often do in the grand old woods in Canada; and so she was soon far, far away from the artful coon, who waited a long time, hoping to carry off poor Silvy for his dinner.

Silvy contrived to pick up a living by digging for roots and eating such fruits as she could find; but one day she came to a grassy cleared spot, where she saw a strange-looking tent, made with poles stuck into the ground and meeting at the top, from which came a bluish cloud that spread among the trees; and as Silvy was very curious, she came nearer, and at last, hearing no sound, ran up one of the poles and peeped in, to see what was within side, thinking it might be one of the fine stores of grain that people built for the squirrels, as her cousin Blackie had made her believe. The poles were covered with sheets of birch-bark and skins of deer and wolves, and there was a fire of sticks burning in the middle, round which some large creatures were sitting on a bear's skin, eating something that smelt very nice. They had long black hair and black eyes and very white teeth. Silvy felt alarmed at first; but thinking they must be the people who were kind to squirrels, she ventured to slip through a slit in the bark, and ran down into the wigwam, hoping to get something to eat; but in a minute the Indians jumped up, and before she had time to make her escape, she was seized by a young squaw, and popped into a birch box, and the lid shut down upon her; so poor Silvy was caught in a trap, and all for believing the artful black squirrel's tales.

Silver-nose remembered her mother's warning now when it was too late; she tried to get out of her prison, but in vain; the sides of the box were too strong, and there was not so much as a single crack for a peep-hole. After she had been shut up some time, the lid was raised a little, and a dark hand put in some bright, shining hard grains for her to eat. This was Indian corn, and it was excellent food; but Silvy was a long, long time before she would eat any of this sweet corn, she was so vexed at being caught and shut up in prison; besides, she was very much afraid that the Indians were going to eat her. After some days, she began to get used to her captive state; the little squaw used to feed her, and one day took her out of the box and put her into a nice light cage, where there was soft green moss to lie on, a little bark dish with clear water, and abundance of food. The cage was hung up on the bough of a tree near the wigwam, to swing to and fro as the wind waved the tree. Here Silvy could see the birds flying to and fro, and listen to their cheerful songs. The Indian women and children had always a kind look or a word to say to her; and

THE PET SQUIRREL.

her little mistress was so kind to her, that Silvy could not help loving her. She was very grateful for her care; for when she was sick and sulky, the little squaw gave her bits of maple-sugar and parched rice out of her hand. At last Silvy grew tame, and would suffer herself to be taken out of her house to sit on her mistress's shoulder or in her lap; and though she sometimes ran away and hid herself, out of fun, she would not have gone far from the tent of the good Indians on any account. Sometimes she saw the red squirrels running about in the forest, but they never came very near her; but she used to watch all day long for her brother Nimble-foot, or sister Velvet-paw; but they were now far away from her, and no doubt thought that she had been killed by the red squirrel, or eaten up by a fox or racoon.

"Nurse, I am so glad pretty Silvy was not killed, and that the good Indians took care of her."

"It is time now, my dear, for you to put down your book," said Mrs. Frazer, "and to-morrow we will read some more."

"Yes, if you please, Mrs. Frazer," said Lady Mary.

Part III.

HOW THE SQUIRRELS GOT TO THE MILL AT THE RAPIDS—AND WHAT HAPPENED TO VELVET-PAW.

NIMBLE-FOOT and Velvet-paw were so frightened by the sight of the red squirrel, that they ran down the tree without once looking back to see what had become of poor Silver-nose; indeed, the cowards, instead of waiting for their poor sister, fled through the forest as if an army of red squirrels were behind them. At last they reached the banks of the lake, and jumping into the water, swam down the current till they came to a place called the "Narrow," where the wide lake poured its waters through a deep rocky channel, not more than a hundred yards wide; here the waters became so rough and rapid, that our little swimmers thought it wisest to go on shore. They scrambled up the steep rocky bank, and found themselves on a wide open space, quite free from trees, which they knew must be one of the great clearings the traveller squirrel had spoken of. There was a very high building on the water's edge that they thought must be the mill that the chitmunks had told them they would come to; and they were in good spirits, as they now expected to find plenty of good things laid up for them to eat, so they went in by the door of the mill.

"Dear me, what a dust there is!" said Nimble, looking about him; "I think it must be snowing."

"Snow does not fall in hot weather," said Velvet; "besides, this white powder is very sweet and nice;" and she began to lick some of the flour that lay in the cracks of the floor.

"I have found some nice seeds here," said Nimble, running to the top of a sack that stood with the mouth untied; "these are better than pine-kernels, and not so hard. We must have come to one of the great grain-stores that our cousin told us of. Well,

I am sure the people are very kind to have laid up so many good things for us squirrels."

When they had eaten as much as they liked, they began to run about to see what was in the mill. Presently, a man came in, and they saw him take one of the sacks of wheat, and pour it into a large upright box, and in a few minutes there was a great noise—a sort of buzzing, whirring, rumbling, dashing, and splashing—and away ran Velvet-paw in a terrible fright, and scrambled up some beams and rafters to the top of the wall, where she sat watching what was going on, trembling all over; but finding that no harm happened to her, took courage, and after a time ceased to be afraid. She saw Nimble perched on a cross-beam looking down very intently at something; so she came out of her corner and ran to him, and asked what he was looking at.

"There is a great black thing here," said he, "I cannot tell what to make of him at all; it turns round, and round, and round, and dashes the water about, making a fine splash." (This was the water-wheel.)

"It looks very ugly indeed," said Velvet-paw, "and makes my head giddy to look at it; let us go away. I want to find out what these two big stones are doing," said she; "they keep rubbing against one another, and making a great noise."

"There is nothing so wonderful in two big stones, my dear," said Nimble; "I have seen plenty bigger than these in Stony Lake."

"But they did not move about as these do; and only look here at the white stuff that is running down all the time into this great box. Well, we shall not want for food for the rest of our lives; I wish poor Silvy were with us to share in our good luck."

They saw a great many other strange things in the mill, and they thought that the miller was a very funny-looking creature; but as they fancied that he was grinding the wheat into flour for them, they were not much afraid of him; they were more troubled at the sight of a black dog, which spied them out as they sat on the beams of the mill, and ran about in a great rage, barking at them in a frightful way, and never left off till the miller went out of the mill, when he went away with his master, and did not return till the next day; but whenever he saw the gray squirrels, this little dog, whose name was "Pinch," was sure to set up his ears and tail, and snap and bark, showing all his sharp white teeth in a very savage manner.

Not far from the mill was another building: this was the house the miller lived in; and close by the house was a barn, a stable, a cow-shed, and a sheep-pen, and there was a garden full of fruit and flowers, and an orchard of apple-trees close by.

One day Velvet-paw ran up one of the apple-trees and began to eat an apple; it looked very good, for it had a bright red cheek, but it was hard and sour, not being ripe. "I do not like these big, sour berries," said she, making wry faces as she tried to get the bad taste out of her mouth by wiping her tongue on her fore-paw. Nimble had found some ripe currants; so he only laughed at poor Velvet for the trouble she was in.

These little gray squirrels now led a merry life; they found plenty to eat and drink, and would not have had a care in the world, if it had not been for the noisy little dog Pinch, who let them have no quiet, barking and baying at them whenever he saw them; and also for the watchful eyes of a great tom-cat, who was always prowling about the mill, or creeping round the orchard and outhouses; so that with all their good food they were not quite free from causes of fear, and no doubt sometimes wished themselves safe back on the little rocky island, in their nest in the old oak-tree.

Time passed away—the wheat and the oats were now ripe and fit for the scythe, for in Canada the settlers mow wheat with an instrument called a "cradle scythe." The beautiful Indian corn was in bloom, and its long pale green silken threads were waving in the summer breeze. The blue jays were busy in the fields of wheat; so were the red-winged blackbirds, and the sparrows, and many other birds, great and small; field-mice in dozens were cutting the straw with their sharp teeth, and carrying off the grain to their nests; and as to the squirrels and chit-munks, there were scores of them—black, red, and gray—filling their cheeks with the grain, and laying it out on the rail fences and on the top of the stumps to dry, before they carried it away to their storehouses. And many a battle the red and the black squirrels had, and sometimes the gray joined with the red, to beat the black ones off the ground.

Nimble-foot and his sister kept out of these quarrels as much as they could; but once they got a severe beating from the red squirrels for not helping them to drive off the saucy black ones, which would carry away the little heaps of wheat, as soon as they were dry.

"We do not mean to trouble ourselves with laying up winter stores," said Nimble one day to his red cousins; "don't you see Peter, the miller's man, has got a great waggon and horses, and is carting wheat into the barn for us?"

The red squirrel opened his round eyes very wide at this speech. "Why, Cousin Nimble," he said, "you are not so foolish as to think the miller is harvesting that grain for your use. No, no, my friend; if you want any, you must work as we do, or run the chance of starving in the winter."

Then Nimble told him what their cousin Blackie had said. "You were wise fellows to believe such nonsense!" said the red squirrel. "These mills and barns are all stored for the use of the miller and his family; and what is more, my friend, I can tell you that men are no great friends to us poor squirrels, and will kill us when they get the chance, and begrudge us the grain we help ourselves to."

"Well, that is very stingy," said Velvet-paw; "I am sure there is enough for men and squirrels too. However, I suppose all must live, so we will let them have what we leave; I shall help myself after they have stored it up in yonder barn."

"You had better do as we do, and make hay while the sun shines," said the red squirrel.

"I would rather play in the sunshine, and eat what I want here," said idle Velvet-paw, setting up her fine tail like a feather over her back, as she ate an ear of corn.

"You are a foolish, idle thing, and will come to no good," said the red squirrel. "I wonder where you were brought up?"

I am very sorry to relate that Velvet-paw did not come to a good end, for she did not take the advice of her red cousin, to lay up provisions during the harvest; but instead of that, she ate all day long, and grew fat and lazy; and after the fields were all cleared, she went to the mill one day, when the mill was grinding, and seeing a quantity of wheat in the feeder of the mill, she ran up a beam and jumped down, thinking to make a good dinner from the grain she saw; but it kept sliding down and sliding down so fast, that she could not get one grain, so at last she began to be frightened, and tried to get up again, but, alas! this was not possible. She cried out to Nimble to help her; and while he ran to look for a stick for her to raise herself up by, the mill-wheel kept on turning, and the great stones went round faster and faster, till poor Velvet-paw was crushed to death between them. Nimble was now left all alone, and sad enough he was, you may suppose.

"Ah," said he, "idleness is the ruin of gray squirrels, as well as men, so I will go away from this place, and try and earn an honest living in the forest. I wish I had not believed all the fine tales my cousin the black squirrel told me."

Then Nimble went away from the clearing, and once more resolved to seek his fortune in the woods. He knew there were plenty of butter-nuts, acorns, hickory-nuts, and beech-nuts, to be found, besides many sorts of berries; and he very diligently set to work to lay up stores against the coming winter.

As it was now getting cold at night, Nimble-foot thought it would be wise to make himself a warm house; so he found out a tall hemlock-pine that was very thick and bushy at the top; there was a forked branch in the tree, with a hollow just fit for his nest. He carried twigs of birch and beech, and over these he laid dry green moss, which he collected on the north side of the cedar trees, and some long gray moss that he found on the swamp maples, and then he stripped the silky threads from the milk-weeds, and the bark of the cedar and birch-trees. These he gnawed fine, and soon made a soft bed; he wove and twisted the sticks, and roots, and mosses together, till the walls of his house were quite thick, and he made a sort of thatch over the top with dry leaves and long moss, with a round hole to creep in and out of.

Making this warm house took him many days' labour; but many strokes will fell great oaks, so at last Nimble-foot's work came to an end, and he had the comfort of a charming house to shelter him from the cold season. He laid up a good store of nuts, acorns, and roots: some he put in a hollow branch of the hemlock-tree close to his nest; some he hid in a stump, and another store he laid under the roots of a mossy cedar. When all this was done, he began to feel very lonely, and often wished, no doubt, that he had had his sisters Silvy and Velvet-paw with him, to share his nice warm house; but of Silvy he knew nothing, and poor Velvet-paw was dead.

One fine moonlight night, as Nimble was frisking about on the bough of a birch-tree, not very far from his house in the hemlock, he saw a canoe land on the shore of the lake, and some Indians with an axe cut down some bushes, and having cleared a small piece of ground, begin to sharpen the ends of some long poles. These they stuck into the ground close together in a circle; and having stripped some sheets of birch-bark from the birch trees close by, they thatched the sides of the hut, and made a fire of sticks inside. They had a dead deer in the canoe, and there were several hares and black squirrels, the sight of which rather alarmed Nimble; for he thought if they killed one sort of squirrel, they might another, and he was very much scared at one of the Indians firing off a gun close by him. The noise made him fall down to the ground, and it was a good thing that it was dark among the leaves and grass where the trunk of the tree threw its long shadow, so that the Indian did not see him, or perhaps he might have loaded the gun again, and shot our little friend, and made soup of him for his supper.

Nimble ran swiftly up a pine-tree, and was soon out of danger. While he was watching some of the Indian children at play, he saw a girl come out of the hut with a gray squirrel in her arms; it did not seem at all afraid of her, but nestled to her shoulder, and even ate out of her hand; and what was Nimble's surprise to see that this tame gray squirrel was none other than his own pretty sister Silver-nose, whom he had left in the hollow tree when they both ran away from the red squirrel.

You may suppose the sight of his lost companion was a joyful one; he waited for a long, long time, till the fire went out, and all the Indians were fast asleep, and little Silvy came out to play in the moonlight, and frisk about on the dewy grass as she used to do. Then Nimble when he saw her, ran down the tree, and came to her and rubbed his nose against her, and licked her soft fur, and told her who he was, and how sorry he was for having left her in so cowardly a manner, to be beaten by the red squirrel.

The good little Silvy told Nimble not to fret

NIMBLE RECOVERING HIS SISTER.

about what was past, and then she asked him for her sister Velvet-paw. Nimble had a long sorrowful tale to tell about the death of poor Velvet; and

Silvy was much grieved. Then in her turn she told Nimble all her adventures, and how she had been caught by the Indian girl, and kept, and fed, and tamed, and had passed her time very happily, if it had not been for thinking about her dear lost companions. "But now," she said, "my dear brother, we will never part again; you shall be quite welcome to share my cage, and my nice stores of Indian corn, rice, and nuts, which my kind mistress gives me."

"I would not be shut up in a cage, not even for one day," said Nimble, "for all the nice fruit and grain in Canada. I am a free squirrel, and love my liberty. I would not exchange a life of freedom in these fine old woods, for all the dainties in the world. So, Silvy, if you prefer a life of idleness and ease to living with me in the forest, I must say good-bye to you."

"But there is nothing to hurt us, my dear Nimble—no racoons, nor foxes, nor hawks, nor owls, nor weasels; if I see any hungry-looking birds or beasts, I have a safe place to run to, and never need be hungry!"

"I would not lead a life like that, for the world," said Nimble. "I should die of dulness; if there is danger in a life of freedom, there is pleasure too, which you cannot enjoy, shut up in a wooden cage, and fed at the will of a master or mistress.—Well, I shall be shot if the Indians awake and see me; so I shall be off."

Silvy looked very sorrowful; she did not like to part from her newly-found brother, but she was unwilling to forego all the comforts and luxuries her life of captivity afforded her.

"You will not tell the Indians where I live, I hope, Silvy, for they would think it a fine thing to hunt me with their dogs, or shoot me down with their bows and arrows."

At these words Silvy was overcome with grief, so jumping off from the log on which she was standing, she said, "Nimble, I will go with you and share all your perils, and we will never part again." She then ran into the wigwam; and going softly to the little squaw, who was asleep, licked her hands and face, as if she would say, "Good-bye, my good kind friend; I shall not forget all your love for me, though I am going away from you for ever."

Silvy then followed Nimble into the forest, and they soon reached his nice comfortable nest in the tall hemlock-tree.

———

"Nurse, I am glad Silvy went away with Nimble; are not you? Poor Nimble must have been so lonely without her; and then you know it must have seemed so hard to him if Silvy had preferred staying with the Indians to living with him."

"Those who have been used to a life of ease do not willingly give it up, my dear lady. Thus you see love for her old companion was stronger even than love of self. But I think you must have tired yourself with reading so long to me."

"Indeed, nurse, I must read a little more, for I want you to hear how Silvy and Nimble amused themselves in the hemlock-tree."

Then Lady Mary continued reading as follows:—

Silvy was greatly pleased with her new home, which was as soft and as warm as clean dry moss, hay, and fibres of roots could make it. The squirrels built a sort of pent or outer roof of twigs, dry leaves, and roots of withered grass, which was pitched so high that it threw off the rain and kept the inner-house very dry. They worked at this very diligently, and also laid up a store of nuts and berries. They knew that they must not only provide plenty of food for the winter, but also for the spring months, when they could get little to eat beside the buds and bark of some sort of trees, and the chance seeds that might still remain in the pine-cones.

Thus the autumn months passed away very quickly and cheerfully with the squirrels while preparing for the coming winter. Half the cold season was spent, too, in sleep; but on mild, sunny days the little squirrels, roused by the bright light of the sunbeams on the white and glittering snow, would shake themselves, rub their black eyes, and after licking themselves clean from dust, would whisk out of their house, and indulge in merry gambols up and down the trunks of the trees, skipping from bough to bough, and frolicking over the hard, crisp snow, which scarcely showed on its surface the delicate print of their tiny feet and the sweep of their fine light feathery tails. Sometimes they met with some little shrewmice running on the snow. These very tiny things are so small, they hardly look bigger than a large black beetle. They lived on the seeds of the tall weeds, which they might be seen climbing and clinging to, yet were hardly heavy enough to weigh down the heads of the dry stalks. It is pretty to see the footprints of these small shrewmice on the surface of the fresh fallen snow in the deep forest glades. They are not dormant during the winter, like many of the mouse tribe, for they are up and abroad at all seasons; for however stormy and severe the weather may be, they do not seem to heed its inclemency. Surely, children, there is One who cares for the small tender things of earth, and shelters them from the rude blasts.

Nimble-foot and Silver-nose often saw their cousins, the black squirrels, playing in the sunshine, chasing each other merrily up and down the trees or over the brush-heaps; their jetty coats and long feathery tails forming a striking contrast with the whiteness of the snow above which they were sporting. Sometimes they saw a few red squirrels too, but there was generally war between them and the black ones.

In these lonely forests everything seems still and silent during the long wintry season, as if death had spread a white pall over the earth, and hushed every living thing into silence. Few sounds are heard through the winter days to break the deathlike silence that reigns around, excepting the sudden rending and cracking of the trees in the frosty air, the fall of a decayed branch, the tapping of a solitary woodpecker—two or three small species of which still remain after all the summer-birds are flown—and the gentle, weak chirp of the little tree-creeper, as it runs up and down the hemlocks and pines, searching the crevices of the bark for insects. Yet in all this seeming death lies hidden the life of myriads of insects, the huge beast of the forest asleep in his lair, with many of the smaller quadrupeds and forest-birds, that, hushed in lonely places, shall awake to life and activity as soon as the sun-beams once more dissolve the snow, unbind the frozen streams, and loosen the bands which held them in repose.

At last the spring, the glad, joyous spring, returned. The leaf-buds, wrapped within their gummy and downy cases, began to unfold; the dark green pines, spruce, and balsams began to shoot out fresh spiny leaves, like tassels, from the ends of every bough, giving out the most refreshing fragrance; the crimson buds of the young hazels and the scarlet blossoms of the soft maple enlivened the edges of the streams; the bright coral bark of the dogwood seemed as if freshly varnished, so brightly it glowed in the morning sunshine; the scream of the blue jay, the song of the robin and woodthrush, the merry note of the chiccadee and plaintive cry of the pheobe, with loud hammering strokes of the great red-headed woodpecker, mingled with the rush of the unbound forest streams, gurgling and murmuring as their water flowed over their stones, and the sighing of the breeze playing in the tree-tops, made pleasant and ceaseless music. And then, as time passed on, the trees unfolded all their bright green leaves—the buds and forest flowers opened; and many a bright bell our little squirrels looked down upon, from their leafy home, that the eye of man had never seen.

It was pleasant for our little squirrels, just after sunset, in the still summer evenings, when the small silver stars came stealing out one by one in the blue sky, to play among the cool dewy leaves of the grand old oaks and maples; to watch the fitful flash of the fireflies, as they glanced here and there, flitting through the deep gloom of the forest boughs, now lost to sight, as they closed their wings, now flashing out like tiny tapers, borne aloft by unseen hands in the darkness. Where that little creek runs singing over its mossy bed, and the cedar-boughs bend down so thick and close that only a gleam of the bright water can be seen, even in the sunlight, there the fireflies crowd, and the damp foliage is all alive with their dazzling light.

In this sweet, still hour, just at the dewfall, the rush of whirring wings may be heard from the islands, or in the forest, bordering on the water's edge; and out of hollow logs and hoary trunks of trees come forth the speckled night-hawks, cutting the air with their thin, sharp, wide wings and open beak, ready to intrap the unwary moth or musquito that float so joyously upon the evening air. One after another, sweeping in wider circles, come forth these birds of prey, till the whole air seems alive with them; darting hither and thither, and uttering wild, shrill screams, as they rise higher and higher in the upper air, till some are almost lost to sight. Sometimes one of them will descend with a sudden swoop to the lower regions of the air, just above the highest tree-tops, with a hollow, booming sound, as if some one were blowing in an empty vessel.

At this hour, too, the bats would quit their homes in hollow trees and old rocky banks, and flit noiselessly abroad over the surface of the quiet, star-lit lake: and now also would begin the shrill, trilling note of the green-frog, and the deep, hoarse bass of the bull-frog, which ceases only at intervals, through the long, warm summer night. You might fancy a droll sort of dialogue was being carried on among them. At first a great fellow, the patriarch of the swamp, will put up his head, which looks very much like a small pair of bellows, with yellow leather sides, and say, in a harsh, guttural tone, "Go to bed, go to bed, go to bed." After a moment's pause, two or three will rise and reply, "No, I won't; no, I won't; no, I won't." Then the old fellow, with a growl, replies, "Get out, get out, get out." And forthwith, with a rush, and a splash, and a dash, they raise a chorus of whirring, grating, growling, grunting, whistling sounds, which make you stop up your ears. When all this hubbub has lasted some minutes, there is a pop and a splash, and down go all the heads under the weeds and mud; and after another pause, up comes the aged father of the frogs, and begins again with the old story, " Go to bed, go to bed, go to bed," and so on. During the heat of the day the bull-frogs are silent; but as the day declines and the air becomes cooler, they recommence their noisy chorus.

I suppose these sounds, though not very pleasant to the ears of men, may not be so disagreeable to those of wild animals. I daresay neither Nimble nor Silvy were in the least annoyed by the hoarse note of the bull-frog, but gambolled as merrily among the boughs and fresh dewy leaves as if they were listening to sweet music or the songs of the birds.

The summer passed away very happily; but towards the close of the warm season the squirrels, Nimble and Silvy, resolved to make a journey to the rocky island on Stony Lake, to see the old squirrels, their father and mother. So they started at sunrise one fine pleasant day, and travelled along; till one cool evening, just as the moon was beginning to rise above the pine-trees, they arrived at the little rocky islet where they first saw the light. But when they eagerly ran up the trunk of the old oak tree, expecting to have seen their old father and mother, they were surprised and terrified by seeing a wood-owl in the nest.

As soon as she espied our little squirrels she shook her feathers and set up her ears—for she was a long-eared owl—and said,—

"What do you want here?—ho, ho, ho, ho!"

"Indeed, Mrs. Owl," said Nimble, "we come hither to see our parents, whom we left here a year ago. Can you tell us where we shall find them?"

The owl peered out of her ruff of silken feathers, and, after wiping her sharp bill on her breast, said,—

"Your cousin, the black squirrel, beat your father and mother out of their nest a long time ago, and took possession of the tree and all that was in it; and they brought up a large family of little ones, all of which I pounced upon one after another, and ate. Indeed, the oaks here belong to my family; so, finding these impudent intruders would not quit the premises, I made short work of the matter, and took the law into my own hands."

"Did you kill them?" asked Silvy, in a trembling voice.

"Of course I did; and very nice, tender meat they were," replied the horrid old owl, beginning to scramble out of the nest, and eyeing the squirrels at the same time with a wicked look.

"But you did not eat our parents too?" asked the trembling squirrels.

"Yes, I did. They were very tough, to be sure; but I am not very particular."

The gray squirrels, though full of grief and vain regret, were obliged to take care of themselves. There was, indeed, no time to be lost; so they made a hasty retreat. They crept under the roots of an old tree, where they lay till the morning. They were not much concerned for the death of the treacherous black squirrel who had told so many stories, got possession of their old nest, and caused the death of their parents; but they said, "We will go home again to our dear old hemlock-tree, and never leave it more." So these dear little squirrels returned to their forest home, and may be living there yet.

"Nurse," said Lady Mary, "how do you like the story?"

Mrs. Frazer said it was a very pretty one.

"Perhaps my dear little pet is one of Nimble or Silvy's children. You know, nurse, they might have gone on their travels too, when they were old enough, and then your brother may have chopped down the tree, and found them in the forest."

"But your squirrel, Lady Mary, is a flying squirrel, and these were only common gray ones, which belong to a different species. Besides, my dear, this history is but a fable."

"I suppose, nurse," said the child, looking up in her nurse's face, "squirrels do not really talk."

"No, my dear; they have not the use of speech as we have. But in all ages people have written little tales called fables, in which they make birds and beasts speak as if they were men and women, it being an easy method of conveying instruction."

"My book is only a fable, then, nurse? I wish it had been true: but it is very pretty."

CHAPTER IV.

SQUIRRELS—THE CHITMUNKS—DOCILITY OF A PET ONE—ROGUERY OF A YANKEE PEDLAR—RETURN OF THE MUSICAL CHITMUNK TO HIS MASTER'S BOSOM—SAGACITY OF A BLACK SQUIRREL.

"MRS. FRAZER, are you very busy just now?" asked Lady Mary, coming up to the table where her nurse was ironing some lace.

"No, my dear, not very busy, only preparing these lace edgings for your frocks. Do you want me to do anything for you?"

"I only want to tell you that my governess has promised to paint my dear squirrel's picture, as soon as it is tame, and will let me hold it in my lap, without flying away. I saw a picture of a flying squirrel to-day, but it was very ugly—not at all like mine; it was long and flat, and its legs looked like sticks, and it was stretched out, just like one of those muskrat skins that you pointed out to me in a fur store. Mamma said it was drawn so, to show it while it was in the act of flying; but it is not pretty—it does not show its beautiful tail, nor its bright eyes, nor soft silky fur. I heard a lady tell mamma about a nest full of dear, tiny little flying squirrels, that her brother once found in a tree in the forest; he tamed them, and they lived very happily together, and would feed from his hand. They slept in the cold weather like dormice; in the daytime they lay very still, but would come out, and gambol and frisk about at night. But somebody left the cage open, and they all ran away except one; and that he found in his bed, where it had run for shelter, with its little nose under his pillow. He caught the little fellow, and it lived with him till the spring, when it grew restless, and one day got away, and went off to the woods."

"These little creatures are impatient of confinement, and will gnaw through the woodwork of the cage to get free, especially in the spring of the year. Doubtless, my dear, they pine for the liberty which they used to enjoy before they were captured by man."

"Nurse, I will not let my little pet be unhappy. As soon as the warm days come again, and my governess has taken his picture, I will let him go free. Are there many squirrels in this part of Canada?"

"Not so many as in Upper Canada, Lady Mary. They abound more in some years than in others. I have seen the beech and oak woods swarming with black squirrels. My brothers have brought in two or three dozen in one day. The Indians used to tell us that want of food, or very severe weather setting in in the north, drive these little animals from their haunts. The Indians, who observe these things more than we do, can generally tell what sort of winter it will be, from the number of wild animals in the fall."

"What do you mean by the fall, nurse?"

"The autumn in Canada, my lady, is called so from the fall of the leaves. I remember one year was remarkable for the great number of black, gray, and flying squirrels; the little striped chitmunk was also plentiful, and so were weasels and foxes. They came into the barns and granaries, and into the houses, and destroyed great quantities of grain; besides gnawing clothes that were laid out to dry; this they did to line their nests with. Next year there were very few to be seen."

"What became of them, nurse?"

"Some, no doubt, fell a prey to their enemies, the cats, foxes, and weasels, which were also very numerous that year; and the rest, perhaps, went back to their own country again."

"I should like to see a great number of these pretty creatures travelling together," said Lady Mary.

"All wild animals, my dear, are more active by night than by day, and probably make their long journeys during that season. The eyes of many animals and birds are so formed, that they see best in the dim twilight, as cats, and owls, and others. Our heavenly Father has fitted all his creatures for the state in which he has placed them."

"Can squirrels swim like otters and beavers, nurse? If they come to a lake or river, can they cross it?"

"I think they can, Lady Mary; for though these creatures are not formed, like the otter, or beaver, or muskrat, to get their living in the water, they are able to swim when necessity requires them to do so. I heard a lady say that she was crossing a lake, between one of the islands and the shore, in a canoe, with a baby on her lap. She noticed a movement on the surface of the water. At first she thought it might be a water-snake, but the servant lad who was paddling the canoe said it was a red squirrel, and he tried to strike it with the paddle; but the little squirrel leaped out of the water to the blade of the paddle, and sprang on the head of the baby, as it lay on her lap; from whence it jumped to her shoulder, and before she had recovered from her surprise, was in the water again, swimming straight for the shore, where it was soon safe in the dark pine woods."

This feat of the squirrel delighted Lady Mary, who expressed her joy at the bravery of the little creature. Besides, she said she had heard that gray squirrels, when they wished to go to a distance in search of food, would all meet together, and collect pieces of bark to serve them for boats, and would set up their broad tails like sails, to catch the wind, and in this way cross large sheets of water.

"I do not think this can be true," observed Mrs.

Frazer; "for the squirrel, when swimming, uses his tail as an oar or rudder to help the motion, the tail lying flat on the surface of the water; nor do these creatures need a boat, for God, who made them, has *given them* the power of swimming at their need."

"Nurse, you said something about a ground squirrel, and called it a chitmunk. If you please, will you tell me something about it, and why it is called by such a curious name?"

"I believe it is the Indian name for this sort of squirrel, my dear. The chitmunk is not so large as the black, red, and gray squirrels. It is marked along the back with black and white stripes; the rest of its fur is a yellowish tawny colour. It is a very playful, lively, cleanly animal, somewhat resembling the dormouse in its habits. It burrows underground. Its nest is made with great care, with many galleries which open at the surface, so that when attacked by an enemy, it can run from one to another for security. For the squirrel has many enemies; all the weasel tribe, cats, and even dogs attack them. Cats kill great numbers. The farmer shows them as little mercy as he does rats and mice, as they are very destructive, and carry off vast quantities of grain, which they store in hollow trees for use. Not contenting themselves with one granary, they have several in case one should fail, or perhaps become injured by accidental causes. Thus do these simple little creatures teach us a lesson of providential care for future events."

"How wise of these little chitmunks to think of such precautions!" said Lady Mary.

"Nay, my dear child, it is God's wisdom, not theirs. These creatures work according to his will; and so they always do what is fittest and best for their own comfort and safety. Man is the only one of God's creatures who disobeys him."

These words made Lady Mary look grave, till her nurse began to talk to her again about the chitmunk.

"It is very easily tamed, and becomes very fond of its master. It will obey his voice, come at a call or a whistle, sit up and beg, take a nut or an acorn out of his hand, run up a stick, nestle in his bosom, and become quite familiar. My uncle had a tame chitmunk that was much attached to him; it lived in his pocket or bosom; it was his companion by day and by night. When he was out in the forest lumbering, or on the lake fishing, or in the fields at work, it was always with him. At meals it sat by the side of his plate, eating what he gave it; but he did not give it meat, as he thought that might injure its health. One day he and his pet were in the steam-boat, going to Toronto. He had been showing off the little chitmunk's tricks to the ladies and gentlemen on board the boat, and several persons offered him money if he would sell it; but my uncle was fond of the little thing, and would not part with it. However, just before he left the boat, he missed his pet; for a cunning Yankee pedlar on board had stolen it. My uncle knew that his little friend would not desert its old master; so he went on deck where the passengers were assembled, and whistled a popular tune familiar to the chitmunk. The little fellow, on hearing it, whisked out of the pedlar's pocket, and running swiftly along a railing against which he was standing, soon sought refuge in his master's bosom."

Lady Mary clapped her hands with joy, and said, "I am so glad, nurse, that the chitmunk ran back to his old friend. I wish it had bitten that Yankee pedlar's fingers."

"When angry these creatures will bite very sharply, set up their tails, and run to and fro, and make a chattering sound with their teeth. The red squirrel is very fearless for its size, and will sometimes turn round and face you, set up its tail, and scold. But they will, when busy eating the seeds of the sunflower or thistle, of which they are very fond, suffer you to stand and watch them without attempting to run away. When near their granaries, or the tree where their nest is, they are unwilling to leave it, running to and fro, and uttering their angry notes; but if a dog is near they make for a tree, and as soon as they are out of his reach, turn round to chatter and scold, as long as he remains in sight. When hard pressed, the black and flying squirrels will take prodigious leaps, springing from bough to bough, and from tree to tree. In this manner they baffle the hunters, and travel a great distance over the tops of the trees. Once I saw my uncle and brothers chasing a large black squirrel. He kept out of reach of the dogs, as well as out of sight of the men, by passing round and round the tree as he went up, so that they could never get a fair shot at him. At last, they got so provoked that they took their axes, and set to work to chop down the tree. It was a large pine tree, and took them some time. Just as the tree was ready to fall, and was wavering to and fro, the squirrel, that had kept on the topmost bough, sprang nimbly to the next tree, and then to another, and by the time the great pine had reached the ground, the squirrel was far away in his nest among his little ones, safe from hunters, guns, and dogs."

"The black squirrel must have wondered, I think, nurse, why so many men and dogs tried to kill such a little creature as he was. Do the black squirrels sleep in the winter as well as the flying squirrels and chitmunks?"

"No, Lady Mary; I have often seen them on bright days chasing each other over logs and brush-heaps, and running gaily up the pine trees. They are easily seen from the contrast which their jetty black coats make with the sparkling white snow. These creatures feed a good deal on the kernels of the pines and hemlocks; they also eat the buds of some trees. They lay up great stores of nuts and grain for winter use. The flying squirrels sleep much, and in the cold season lie heaped upon each other, for the sake of warmth. As many as seven or eight may be found in one nest asleep. They sometimes awaken, if there come a succession of warm days, as in the January thaw; for I must tell you that in this country we generally have rain and mild weather for a few days in the beginning of January, when the snow nearly disappears from the ground. About the 12th, the weather sets in again steadily cold; when the little animals retire once more to sleep in their winter cradles, which they rarely leave till the hard weather is over."

"I suppose, nurse, when they awake, they are glad to eat some of the food they have laid up in their granaries?"

"Yes, my dear, it is for this they gather their hoards in mild weather; which also supports them in the spring months, and possibly even during the summer, till grain and fruit are ripe. I was walking in the harvest field one day, where my brothers were cradling wheat. As I passed along the fence, I noticed a great many little heaps of wheat lying here and there on the rails, also upon the tops of the stumps in the field. I wondered at first who could have placed them there, but presently noticed a number of red squirrels running very swiftly along the fence, and perceived that they emptied their mouths of a quantity of the new wheat, which they had been diligently employed in collecting from the ears that lay scattered over the ground. These little gleaners did not seem to be at all alarmed at my presence, but went to and fro as busy as bees. On taking some of the grains into my hand, I noticed that the germ or eye of the kernels was bitten clean out."

"What was that for, nurse? can you tell me?"

"My dear young lady, I did not know at first, till, upon showing it to my father, he told me that the squirrels destroyed the germ of the grain, such as wheat or Indian corn, that they stored up for winter use, that it might not sprout when buried in the ground or in a hollow tree."

"This is very strange, nurse," said the little girl. "But I suppose," she added, after a moment's thought, "it was God who taught the squirrels to do so. But why would biting out the eye prevent the grain from growing?"

"Because the eye or bud contains the life of the plant; from it springs the green blade, and the stem that bears the ear, and the root that strikes down to the earth. The flowery part, which swells and becomes soft and jelly-like, serves to nourish the young plant till the tender fibres of the roots are able to draw moisture from the ground."

Lady Mary asked if all seeds had an eye or germ.

Her nurse replied that all had, though some were so minute that they looked no bigger than dust, or a grain of sand; yet each was perfect in its kind, and contained the plant that would, when sown in the earth, bring forth roots, leaves, buds, flowers, and fruits in due season.

"How glad I should have been to see the little squirrels gleaning the wheat, and laying it in the little heaps on the rail fence. Why did they not carry it at once to their nests?"

"They laid it out in the sun and wind to dry; for if it had been stored away while damp, it would have moulded, and have been spoiled. The squirrels were busy all that day; when I went to see them again, the grain was gone. I saw several red squirrels running up and down a large pine tree, which had been broken by the wind at the top; and there, no doubt, they had laid up stores. These squirrels did not follow each other in a straight line, but ran round and round in a spiral direction, so that they never hindered each other, nor came in each other's way: two were always going up, while the other two were going down. They seem to work in families; for the young ones, though old enough to get their own living, usually inhabit the same nest, and help to store up the grain for winter use. They all separate again in spring. The little chitmunk does not live in trees, but burrows in the ground, or makes its nest in some large hollow log. It is very pretty to see the little chitmunks, on a warm spring day, running about and chasing each other among the moss and leaves; they are not bigger than mice, but look bright and lively. The fur of all the squirrel tribe is used in trimming, but the gray is the best and most valuable. It has often been remarked by the Indians, and others, that the red and black squirrels never live in the same place; for the red, though the smallest, beat away the black ones. The flesh of the black squirrel is very good to eat; the Indians also eat the red."

Lady Mary was very glad to hear all these things, and quite forgot to play with her doll. "Please, Mrs. Frazer," said the little lady, "tell me now about beavers and muskrats." But Mrs. Frazer was obliged to go out on business; she promised, however, to tell Lady Mary all she knew about these animals another day.

CHAPTER V.

INDIAN BASKETS—THREAD PLANTS—MAPLE SUGAR-TREE—
INDIAN ORNAMENTAL WORKS—RACOONS.

IT was some time before Lady Mary's nurse could tell her any more stories. She received a letter from her sister-in-law, informing her that her brother was dangerously ill, confined to what was feared would prove his death-bed, and that he earnestly desired to see her before he died. The Governor's lady, who was very kind and good to all her household, readily consented to let Mrs. Frazer go to her sick relation.

Lady Mary parted from her dear nurse, whom she loved very tenderly, with much regret. Mrs. Frazer told her that it might be a fortnight before she could return, as her brother lived on the shores of one of the small lakes, near the head waters of the Otonabee river, a great way off; but she promised to return as soon as she could, and, to console her young mistress for her absence, promised to bring her some Indian toys from the backwoods.

The month of March passed away pleasantly, for Lady Mary enjoyed many delightful sleigh-drives with her papa and mamma, who took every opportunity to instruct and amuse her. On entering her nursery one day, after enjoying a long drive in the country, great was her joy to find her good nurse sitting quietly at work by the stove. She was dressed in deep mourning, and looked much thinner and paler than when she had last seen her.

The kind little girl knew, when she saw her nurse's black dress, that her brother must be dead; and with the thoughtfulness of a true lady, remained very quiet, and did not annoy her with questions about trifling matters: she spoke low and gently to her, and tried to comfort her when she saw large tears falling on the work which she held in her hand, and kindly said, "Mrs. Frazer, you had better lie down and rest yourself, for you must be tired after your long, long journey."

The next day Mrs. Frazer seemed to be much better; and she showed Lady Mary an Indian basket made of birch-bark, very richly wrought with coloured porcupine-quills, and which had two lids.

Lady Mary admired the splendid colours, and strange patterns on the basket.

"It is for you, my dear," said her nurse; "open it, and see what is in it." Lady Mary lifted one of the lids, and took out another small basket, of a different shape and pattern. It had a top, which was sewn down with coarse-looking thread, which her nurse told her was nothing but the sinews of the deer, dried and beaten fine, and drawn out like thread.

Then, taking an end of it in her hand, she made Lady Mary observe that these coarse threads could be separated into a great number of finer ones, sufficiently delicate to pass through the eye of a fine needle, or to string tiny beads.

"The Indians, my lady, sew with the sinews of the wild animals they kill. These sinews are much stronger and tougher than thread, and therefore are well adapted to sew together such things as moccasins, leggings, and garments made of the skins of wild animals. The finer threads are used for sewing the beads and quill ornaments on moccasins, sheaths, and pouches, besides other things that I cannot now think of.

"Oh yes, I must tell you one thing more they make with these sinews. How do you think the Indian women carry their infants when they go on a long journey? They tie them to a board, and wrap them up in strong bandages of linen or cotton, which they sew firmly together with their stoutest thread, and then they suspend the odd-looking burden to their backs. By this contrivance, they lessen the weight of the child considerably, and are able to walk many miles without showing signs of fatigue. It is also much more pleasant and healthy for the child than to be uncomfortably cramped up in its mother's arms, and shifted about from side to side, as first one arm aches, and then the other.

"The Indian women sew some things with the roots of the tamarack, or larch; such as coarse birch-

INDIAN SQUAW AND BABY.

baskets, bark canoes, and the covering of their wigwams. They call this 'wah-tap'* (wood-thread),

* Asclepia parviflora.

and they prepare it by pulling off the outer rind and steeping it in water. It is the larger fibres which have the appearance of small cordage when coiled up and fit for use. This 'wah-tap' is very valuable to these poor Indians. There is also another plant, called Indian hemp, which is a small shrubby kind of milk-weed, that grows on gravelly islands. It bears white flowers, and the branches are long and slender; under the bark there is a fine silky thread covering the wood; this is tough, and can be twisted and spun into cloth. It is very white and fine, and does not easily break. There are other plants of the same family, with pods full of fine shining silk; but these are too brittle to spin into thread. This last kind, Lady Mary, which is called Milk-weed flytrap, I will show you in summer."*

But while Mrs. Frazer was talking about these plants, the little lady was examining the contents of the small birch-box. "If you please, nurse, will you tell me what these dark shining seeds are?"

"These seeds, my dear, are Indian rice; an old squaw, Mrs. Peter Noggan, gave me this as a present for 'Governor's daughter;'" and Mrs. Frazer imitated the soft, whining tone of the Indian, which made Lady Mary laugh.

"The box is called a 'mowkowk.' There is another just like it, only there is a white bird—a snow-bird, I suppose it is intended for—worked on the lid." The lid of this box was fastened down

* Asclepia Syriaca.

with a narrow slip of deer-skin; Lady Mary cut the fastening, and raised the lid—"Nurse, it is only yellow sand; how droll, to send me a box of sand!"

"It is not sand; taste it, Lady Mary."

"It is sweet—it is sugar! Ah! now I know what it is that this kind old squaw has sent me; it is maple-sugar, and is very nice. I will go and show it to mamma."

"Wait a little, Lady Mary; let us see what there is in the basket besides the rice and the maple-sugar."

"What a lovely thing this is, dear nurse! what can it be?"

"It is a sheath for your scissors, my dear; it is made of doe-skin, embroidered with white beads, and coloured quills split fine, and sewn with deer-sinew thread. Look at these curious bracelets."

Lady Mary examined the bracelets, and said she thought they were wrought with beads; but Mrs. Frazer told her that what she took for beads were porcupine quills, cut out very finely, and strung in a pattern. They were not only neatly but tastefully made; the pattern, though a Grecian scroll, having been carefully imitated by some Indian squaw.

"This embroidered knife-sheath is large enough for a hunting-knife," said Lady Mary, "a '*couteau de chasse*,'—is it not?"

"This sheath was worked by the wife of Isaac Iron, an educated chief of the Mud Lake Indians; she gave it to me because I had been kind to her in sickness."

"I will give it to my dear papa," said Lady

Mary, "for I never go out hunting, and do not wish to carry a large knife by my side;" and she laid the sheath away, after having admired its gay colours, and particularly the figure of a little animal worked in black and white quills, which was intended to represent a racoon.

"This is a present for your doll; it is a doll's mat, woven by a little girl, aged seven years, Rachel Muskrat; and here is a little canoe of red cedar, made by a little Indian boy."

"What a darling little boat! and there is a fish carved on the paddles." This device greatly pleased Lady Mary, who said she would send Rachel a wax doll, and little Moses a knife or some other useful article, when Mrs. Frazer went again to the Lakes; but when her nurse took out of the other end of the basket a birch-bark cradle, made for her doll, worked very richly, she clapped her hands for joy, saying, "Ah, nurse, you should not have brought me so many pretty things at once, for I am too happy!"

The remaining contents of the basket consisted of seeds and berries, and a small cake of maple-sugar, which Mrs. Frazer had made for the young lady. This was very different in appearance from the Indian sugar; it was bright and sparkling, like sugar-candy, and tasted sweeter. The other sugar was dry, and slightly bitter: Mrs. Frazer told Lady Mary that this peculiar taste was caused by the birch-bark vessels, which the Indians used for catching the sap, as it flowed from the maple-trees.

"I wonder who taught the Indians how to make maple-sugar?" asked the child.

"I do not know," replied the nurse. "I have heard that they knew how to make this sugar when the discoverers of the country found them.* It may be that they found it out by accident. The sugar-maple when wounded in March or April, yields a great deal of sweet liquor. Some Indians may have supplied themselves with this juice, when pressed for want of water; for it flows so freely in warm days in spring, that several pints can be obtained from one tree in the course of the day. By boiling this juice, it becomes very sweet; and at last when all the thin watery part has gone off in steam, it becomes thick, like honey; by boiling it still longer, it turns to sugar, when cold. So you see, my dear, that the Indians may have found it out by boiling some sap, instead of water, and letting it remain on the fire till it grew thick."

"Are there many kinds of maple-trees, that sugar can be made from, nurse?" asked the little girl.

"Yes,† my lady; but I believe the sugar-maple yields the best sap for the purpose; that of the birch-tree, I have heard, can be made into sugar; but it would require a larger quantity; weak wine, or vinegar, is made by the settlers of birch-sap,

---

* However this may be, the French settlers claim the merit of converting the sap into sugar.

† All the maple tribe are of a saccharine nature. Sugar has been made in England from the sap of the sycamore.

which is very pleasant tasted. The people who live in the backwoods, and make maple-sugar, always make a keg of vinegar at the sugaring off."

"That must be very useful; but if the sap is sweet, how can it be made into such sour stuff as vinegar?"

Then nurse tried to make Lady Mary understand that the heat of the sun, or of a warm room, would make the liquor ferment, unless it had been boiled a long time, so as to become very sweet, and somewhat thick. The first fermentation, she told her, would give only a winy taste; but if it continued to ferment a great deal, it turned sour, and became vinegar.

"How very useful the maple-tree is, nurse! I wish there were maples in the garden, and I would make sugar, molasses, wine, and vinegar; and what else would I do with my maple-tree?"

Mrs. Frazer laughed, and said,—"The wood makes excellent fuel; but is also used in making bedsteads, chests of drawers, and many other things. There is a very pretty wood for furniture, called 'bird's-eye maple;' the drawers in my bedroom that you think so pretty are made of it; but it is a disease in the tree that causes it to have these little marks all through the wood. In autumn, this tree improves the forest landscape, for the bright scarlet leaves of the maple give a beautiful look to the woods in the fall. The red or soft maple (*Acer rubrus*), another species, is very bright when the leaves are changing, but it gives no sugar."

"Then I will not let it grow in my garden, nurse!"

"It is good for other purposes, my dear. The settlers use the bark for dyeing wool; and a jet black ink can be made from it, by boiling down the bark with a bit of copperas, in an iron vessel; so you see it is useful. The bright red flowers of this tree look very pretty in the spring; it grows best by the water-side, and some call it 'the swamp-maple.'"

This was all Mrs. Frazer could tell Lady Mary about the maple-trees. Many little girls, as young as the Governor's daughter, would have thought it very dull to listen to what her nurse had to say about plants and trees; but Lady Mary would put aside her dolls and toys, to stand beside her to ask questions, and listen to her answers; the more she heard the more she desired to hear, about these things. "The hearing ear, and the seeing eye, are two things that are never satisfied," saith the wise king Solomon.

Lady Mary was delighted with the contents of her Indian basket, and spent the rest of her play-hours in looking at the various articles it contained, and asking her nurse questions about the materials of which they were made. Some of the bark-boxes were lined with paper, but the doll's cradle was not, and Lady Mary perceived that the inside of it was very rough, caused by the hard ends of the quills with which it was ornamented. At first she could not think how the squaws worked with the quills, as they could not possibly thread them through the eye of a needle; but her nurse told her that when they want to work any pattern in birch-bark, they trace it with some sharp-pointed instrument, such as a nail, or bodkin, or even a sharp thorn, with which they pierce holes close together round the edge of the leaf, or blade, or bird they have drawn out on the birch-bark; into these holes they insert one end of the quill, the other end is then drawn through the opposite hole, pulled tight, bent a little, and cut off on the inside. This any one of my young readers may see, if they examine the Indian baskets or toys, made of birch-bark. "I have seen the squaws in their wigwams at work on these things, sitting cross-legged on their mats,—some had the quills in a little bark dish on their laps, while others held them in their mouths—not a very safe nor delicate way; but Indians are not very nice in some of their habits," said Mrs. Frazer. "The prettiest sort of Indian work is done in coloured moose-hair, with which, formed into a sort of rich embroidery, they ornament the moccasins, hunting-knife, sheaths, and birch-bark baskets and toys."

"Nurse, if you please, will you tell me what this little animal is designed to represent?" said Lady Mary, pointing to the figure of the racoon worked in quills on the sheath of the hunting-knife.

"It is intended for a racoon, my lady," replied her nurse.

"Is the racoon a pretty creature like my squirrel?"

"It is much larger than your squirrel; its fur is

not nearly so soft or so fine; the colour being black and gray, or dun; the tail barred across, and bushy,—you have seen many sleigh-robes made of racoon-skins, with the tails looking like tassels at the back of the sleighs."

"Oh yes, and a funny, cunning-looking face peeping out too!"

"The face of this little animal is sharp, and the eyes black and keen, like a fox; the feet bare, like the soles of our feet, only black and leathery; their claws are very sharp; they can climb trees very fast. During the winter the racoons sleep in hollow trees, and cling together for the sake of keeping each other warm. The choppers find as many as seven or eight in one nest, fast asleep. Most probably the young family remain with the old ones until spring, when they separate. The racoon in its habits is said to resemble the bear; like the bear, it lives chiefly on vegetables, especially Indian corn, but I do not think that it lays by any store for winter. They sometimes awake if there come a few warm days, but soon retire again to their warm, cozy nests."

"Racoons will eat eggs; and fowls are often taken by them,—perhaps this is in the winter, when they wake up and are pressed by hunger."

Her nurse said that one of her friends had a racoon which he kept in a wooden cage, but he was obliged to have a chain and collar to keep him from getting away, as he used to gnaw the bars asunder; and had slily stolen away and killed some ducks, and was almost as mischievous as a fox, but was very lively and amusing in his way.

Lady Mary now left her good nurse, and took her basket, with all its Indian treasures, to show to her mamma, with whom we leave her for the present.

CHAPTER VI.

CANADIAN BIRDS—SNOW SPARROW—ROBIN REDBREAST—
CANADIAN FLOWERS—AMERICAN PORCUPINE.

"SPRING is coming, nurse — spring is coming at last!" exclaimed the Governor's little daughter, joyfully. "The snow is going away at last! I am tired of the white snow; it makes my eyes ache. I want to see the brown earth, and the grass, and the green moss, and the pretty flowers again."

"It will be some days before this deep covering of snow is gone. The streets are still slippery with ice, which it will take some time, my lady, to soften."

"But, nurse, the sun shines, and there are little streams of water running along the streets in every direction. See, the snow is gone from under the bushes and trees in the garden. I saw some dear little birds flying about, and I watched them perching on the dry stalks of the tall, rough weeds, and they appeared to be picking seeds out of the husks. Can you tell me what birds they were?"

"I saw the flock of birds you mean, Lady Mary.

THE SNOW-SPARROWS.

WATCHING THE BIRDS.

They are the common snow-sparrows *—almost our earliest visitants, for they may be seen in April, mingled with the brown song-sparrow,† flitting

* Fringilla nivalis. † Fringilla melodia.

about the garden fences, or picking the stalks of the tall mullein and amaranths, to find the seeds that have not been shaken out by the autumn winds; and possibly they also find insects cradled in the husks of the old seed-vessels. These snow-sparrows are very hardy; and though some migrate to the States in the beginning of winter, a few stay in the Upper Province, and others come back to us before the snow is all gone."

"They are very pretty, neat-looking birds, nurse; dark slate colour, with white breasts."

"When I was a little girl I used to call them my Quaker-birds, they looked so neat and prim. In the summer you may find their nests in the brush-heaps near the edge of the forest. They sing a soft, low song."

"Nurse, I heard a bird singing yesterday when I was in the garden; a little, plain, brown bird, nurse."

"It was a song-sparrow, Lady Mary. This cheerful little bird comes with the snow-birds, often before the robin."

"Oh, nurse, the robin! I wish you would show me a darling robin redbreast. I did not know they lived in Canada."

"The bird that we call the robin in this country, my dear, is not like the little redbreast you have seen at home. Our robin is twice as large. Though in shape resembling the European robin, I believe it is really a kind of thrush.* It migrates in the fall, and returns to us early in the spring."

* Turdus migratoria.

"What is migrating, nurse? Is it the same as emigrating?"

"Yes, Lady Mary; for when a person leaves his native country, and goes to live in another country, he is said to emigrate. This is the reason why the English, Scotch, and Irish families who come to live in Canada are called emigrants."

"What colour are the Canadian robins, nurse?"

"The head is blackish; the back, lead colour; and the breast is pale orange — not so bright a red, however, as the real robin."

"Have you ever seen their nests, nurse?"

"Yes, my dear, many of them. It is not a pretty nest. It is large, and coarsely put together, of old dried grass, roots, and dead leaves, plastered inside with clay, mixed with bits of straw, so as to form a sort of mortar. You know, Lady Mary, that the blackbird and thrush build nests, and plaster them in this way?"

The little lady nodded her head in assent.

"Nurse, I once saw a robin's nest when I was in England. It was in the side of a mossy ditch, with primroses growing close beside it. It was made of green moss, and lined with white wool and hair. It was a pretty nest, with nice eggs in it; much better than your Canadian robin's nest."

"Our robins build in upturned roots, in the corners of rail fences, and in the young pear-trees and apple-trees in the orchard. The eggs are a greenish-blue. The robin sings a full, clear song;

indeed, he is our best songster. We have so few singing-birds that we prize those that do sing very much."

"Does the Canadian robin come into the house in winter, and pick up the crumbs, as the dear little redbreasts do at home?"

"No, Lady Mary; they are able to find plenty of food abroad when they return to us, but they hop about the houses and gardens pretty freely. In the fall, before they go away, they may be seen in great numbers, running about the old pastures, picking up worms and seeds."

"Do people see the birds flying away together, nurse?"

"Not often, my dear; for most birds congregate together in small flocks, and depart unnoticed. Many go away at night, when we are sleeping; and some fly very high on cloudy days, so that they are not distinctly seen against the dull, gray sky. The water-birds—such as geese, swans, and ducks—take their flight in large bodies. They are heard making a continual noise in the air; and may be seen grouped in long lines, or in the form of the letter V lying on its side ($>$), the point generally directed southward or westward, the strongest and oldest birds acting as leaders. When tired, these aquatic generals fall backward into the main body, and are replaced by others."

Lady Mary was much surprised at the order and sagacity displayed by wild-fowl in their flight; and

Mrs. Frazer told her that some other time she would tell her some more facts respecting their migration to other countries.

"Nurse, will you tell me something about birds' nests, and what they make them of?"

"Birds that live chiefly in the depths of the forest, or in solitary places, far away from the haunts of men, build their nests of ruder materials, and with less care in the manner of putting them together. Dried grass, roots, and a little moss, seem to be the materials they make use of. It has been noticed by many persons, my dear, that those birds that live near towns and villages and cleared farms, soon learn to make better sorts of nests, and to weave into them soft and comfortable things, such as silk, wool, cotton, and hair."

"That is very strange, nurse."

"It is so, Lady Mary; but the same thing may also be seen among human beings. The savage nations are contented with rude dwellings made of sticks and cane, covered with skins of beasts, bark, or reeds; but when they once unite together in a more social state, and live in villages and towns, a desire for improvement takes place. The tent of skins or the rude shanty is exchanged for a hut of better shape; and this in time gives place to houses and furniture of more useful and ornamental kinds."

"Nurse, I heard mamma say that the Britons who lived in England were once savages, and lived in caves, huts, and thick woods; that they dressed in skins, and painted their bodies like the Indians."

"When you read the history of England, you will see that such was the case," said Mrs. Frazer.

"Nurse, perhaps the little birds like to see the flowers, and the sunshine, and the blue sky, and men's houses. I will make my garden very pretty this spring, and plant some nice flowers, to please the dear little birds."

Many persons would have thought such remarks very foolish in our little lady. But Mrs. Frazer, who was a good and wise woman, did not laugh at the little girl; for she thought it was a lovely thing to see her wish to give happiness to the least of God's creatures, for it was imitating his own goodness and mercy, which delight in the enjoyment of the things which he has called into existence.

"Please, Mrs. Frazer, will you tell me which flowers will be first in bloom?"

"The very first is a plant that comes up without leaves."

"Nurse, that is the Christmas-rose.* I have seen it in the old country."

"No, Lady Mary; it is the colt's-foot.† It is a common-looking, coarse, yellow-blossomed flower: it is the first that blooms after the snow. Then comes the pretty snow-flower, or hepatica. Its pretty tufts of white, pink, or blue starry flowers may be seen on the open clearing, or beneath the

---
* Winter Aconite. † Tussilago farfara.

shade of the half-cleared woods or upturned roots and sunny banks. Like the English daisy, it grows everywhere, and the sight of its bright starry blossoms delights every eye. The next flower that comes in is the dog's-tooth-violet."*

"What a droll name!" exclaimed Lady Mary, laughing.

"I suppose it is called so from the sharpness of the flower-leaves (petals), my lady; but it is a beautiful yellow lily. The leaves are also pretty; they are veined or clouded with milky white or dusky purple. The plant has a bulbous root, and in the month of April sends up its single, nodding, yellow-spotted flowers. They grow in large beds, where the ground is black, moist, and rich, near creeks on the edge of the forest."

"Do you know any other pretty flowers, nurse?"

"Yes, my lady; there are a great many that bloom in April and May: white violets, and blue and yellow of many kinds. And then there is the spring beauty,† a delicate little flower, with pink striped bells; and the everlasting flower; ‡ and saxifrage; and the white and dark red lily, that the Yankees call 'white and red death.' § These have three green leaves about the middle of the stalk, and the flower is composed of three pure white or deep red leaves—petals my father used to call them: for my father, Lady Mary, was a botanist, and knew

---

* Erythronium.   ‡ Graphalium.
† Claytonia.   § Trillium, or Wake Robin.

the names of all the flowers, and I learned them from him. The most curious is the moccasin flower. The early one is bright golden yellow, and has a bag or sack which is curiously spotted with ruby red, and its petals are twisted like horns. There is a hard, thick piece that lies down just above the sack or moccasin part; and if you lift this up, you see a pair of round, dark spots like eyes, and the Indians say it is like the face of a hound, with the nose and black eyes plain to be seen. Two of the shorter, curled, brown petals look like flapped ears, one on each side of the face. There is a more beautiful sort, purple and white, which blooms in August. The plant is taller, and bears large, lovely flowers."

"And has it a funny face and ears too, nurse?"

"Yes, my dear; but the face is more like an ape's: it is even more distinct than in the yellow moccasin. When my brother and I were children, we used to fold back the petals, and call them baby flowers: the sack, we thought, looked like a baby's white frock."

Lady Mary was much amused at this notion.

"There are a great number of very beautiful and also very curious flowers growing in the forest," said Mrs. Frazer. "Some of them are used in medicine, and some by the Indians for dyes, with which they stain the baskets and porcupine quills. One of our earliest flowers is called the blood-root.* It comes up a delicate, white-folded bud, within a vine-shaped

* Sanguivaria.

leaf, which is veined on the under side with orange yellow. If the stem or the root of this plant be broken, a scarlet juice drops out very fast. It is with this the squaws dye red and orange colours."

"I am glad to hear this, nurse. Now I can tell my dear mamma what the baskets and quills are dyed with."

"The flower is very pretty, like a white crocus, only not so large. You saw some crocuses in the conservatory the other day, I think, my dear lady."

"Oh yes; yellow ones, and purple too, in a funny china thing, with holes in its back, and the flowers came up through the holes. The gardener said it was a porcupine.

"Please, nurse, tell me of what colours real porcupine quills are?"

"They are white and grayish-brown."

Then Lady Mary brought a print and showed it to her nurse, saying,—

"Nurse, is the porcupine like this picture?"

"The American porcupine, my dear, is not so large as this species: its spines are smaller and weaker. It resembles the common hedgehog more nearly. It is an innocent animal, feeding mostly on roots * and small fruits. It burrows in dry, stony hillocks, and passes the cold weather in sleep. It goes abroad chiefly during the night.

* There is a plant of the lily tribe, upon whose roots the porcupine feeds, as well as on wild bulbs and berries, and the bark of the black spruce and larch. It will also eat apples and Indian corn.

The spines of the Canadian porcupine are much weaker than those of the African species. The Indians trap these creatures, and eat their flesh. They bake them in their skins in native ovens—holes made in the earth, lined with stones, which they make very hot, covering them over with embers."

Mrs. Frazer had told Lady Mary all she knew about the porcupine, when Campbell, the footman, came to say that her papa wanted to see her.

CHAPTER VII.

INDIAN BAG — INDIAN EMBROIDERY — BEAVER'S TAIL — BEAVER ARCHITECTURE — HABITS OF THE BEAVER — BEAVER TOOLS — BEAVER MEADOWS.

WHEN Lady Mary went down to her father, he presented her with a beautiful Indian bag, which he had brought from Lake Huron, in the Upper Province. It was of fine doe-skin, very nicely wrought with dyed moose-hair, and the pattern was very pretty; the border was of scarlet feathers on one side, and blue on the other, which formed a rich silken fringe at each edge. This was a present from the wife of a chief on Manitoulin Island. Lady Mary was much delighted with her present, and admired this new-fashioned work in moose-hair very much. The feathers, Mrs. Frazer told her, were from the summer red-bird or war-bird, and the blue-bird, both of which Lady Mary said she had seen. The Indians use these feathers as ornaments for their heads and shoulders on grand occasions.

Lady Mary recollected hearing her mamma speak of Indians who wore mantles and dresses of gay

THE PRESENT FROM FATHER.

feathers. They were chiefs of the Sandwich Islands, she believed, who had these superb habits.

"You might tell me something about these Indians, nurse," said little Mary.

"I might occupy whole days in describing their singular customs, my dear," replied Mrs. Frazer, "and I fear you would forget one half of what I told you. But there are numerous interesting books in reference to them, which you will read as you grow older. You would be much amused at the appearance of an Indian chief, when dressed out in the feathers we have been speaking of; his face covered with red paint; his robe flowing loose and free; and his calumet, or pipe, gaily decked with ribbons. The Indians are great orators, being distinguished by their graceful gestures, their animated air, and their vigorous and expressive style. They are tall, well-made, and athletic; their complexion of a reddish copper colour; their hair long, coarse, and jet-black. Their senses are remarkably acute, and they can see and hear with extraordinary distinctness. They will follow up the track of a man or animal through the dense woods and across the vast plains by trifling signs, which no European can detect. Their temperament is cold and unimpassioned; they are capable of enduring extreme hunger and thirst, and seem almost insensible to pain. Under certain circumstances they are generous and hospitable, but when once roused, their vengeance is not easily satisfied. They will pursue a real or supposed foe with a hatred which never tires, and gratify their lust of cruelty by exposing him, when captured, to the most hor-

INDIAN CHIEF ADDRESSING HIS TRIBE.

rible torments. They support themselves by fishing and on the spoils of the chase; and though a few tribes have become partially civilized, and devoted themselves to the peaceful pursuits of husbandry, the majority retire further and further into the dense forests of the west as the white man continues his advance, and wander, like their forefathers, about the lonely shores of the great lakes, and on the banks of the vast rolling rivers."

"Thank you, nurse; I will not forget what you have told me. And now, have you anything more to say about birds and flowers? I can never weary of hearing about such interesting objects."

"I promised to tell you about the beavers, my lady," replied Mrs. Frazer.

"Oh yes, about the beavers that make the dams and the nice houses, and cut down whole trees. I am glad you can tell me something about those curious creatures; for mamma bought me a pretty picture, which I will show you, if you please," said the little girl. "But what is this odd-looking, black thing here? Is it a dried fish? It must be a black bass. Yes, nurse, I am sure it is."

The nurse smiled, and said: "It is not a fish at all, my dear; it is a dried beaver's tail. I brought it from the back lakes when I was at home, that you might see it. See, my lady, how curiously the beaver's tail is covered with scales; it looks like some sort of black leather, stamped in a diaper pattern. Before it is dried it is very heavy, weighing three or four pounds. I have heard my brothers and some of the Indian trappers say, that the animal makes use of its tail to beat the sides of the dams and smooth the mud and clay, as a plasterer uses a trowel. Some people think otherwise, but it seems well suited from its shape and weight for the purpose, and, indeed, as the walls they raise seem to have been smoothed by some implement, I see no reason to disbelieve the story."

"And what do the beavers make dams with, nurse?"

"With small trees cut into pieces, and drawn in close to each other; and then the beavers fill the spaces between with sods, and stones, and clay, and all sorts of things, that they gather together and work up into a solid wall. The walls are made broad at the bottom, and are several feet in thickness, to make them strong enough to keep the water from washing through them. The beavers assemble together in the fall, about the months of October and November, to build their houses and repair their dams. They prefer running water, as it is less likely to freeze. They work in large parties, sometimes fifty or a hundred together, and do a great deal in a short time. They work during the night."

"Of what use is the dam, nurse?"

"The dam is for the purpose of securing a constant supply of water, without which they could not live. When they have enclosed the beaver-pond, they separate into family parties of eleven or twelve, perhaps more, sometimes less, and construct dwellings, which are raised against the inner walls of the dam. These little huts have two chambers, one in

A REMARKABLE EDIFICE. 125

BEAVERS MAKING A DAM.

which they sleep, which is warm and soft and dry, lined with roots and sedges and dry grass, and any odds and ends that serve their purpose. The feeding place is below; in this is stored the wood or the bark on which they feed. The entrance to this is under water, and hidden from sight; but it is there that the cunning hunter sets his trap to catch the unsuspecting beavers.

"A beaver's house is large enough to allow two men a comfortable sleeping-room, and it is kept very clean. It is built of sticks, stones, and mud, and is well plastered outside and in. The trowel the beaver uses in plastering is his tail; this is considered a great delicacy at the table. Their beds are made of chips, split as fine as the brush of an Indian broom; these are disposed in one corner, and kept dry and sweet and clean. It is the bark of the green wood that is used by the beavers for food; after the stick is peeled, they float it out at a distance from the house. Many good housewives might learn a lesson of neatness and order from the humble beaver.

"In large lakes and rivers the beavers make no dams; they have water enough without putting themselves to that trouble; but in small creeks they dam up, and make a better stop-water than is done by the millers. The spot where they build their dams is the most labour-saving place in the valley, and where the work will stand best. When the dam is finished, not a drop of water escapes; their work is always well done."

"Nurse, do not beavers, and otters, and musk-rats feel cold while living in the water; and do they not get wet?"

"No, my dear; they do not feel cold, and cannot get wet, for the thick coating of hair and down keeps them warm; and these animals, like ducks and geese, and all kinds of water-fowls, are supplied with a bag of oil, with which they dress their coats, and that throws off the moisture; for you know, Lady Mary, that oil and water will not mix. All creatures that live in the water are provided with oily fur, or smooth scales, that no water can penetrate; and water-birds, such as ducks and geese, have a little bag of oil, with which they dress their feathers."

"Are there any beavers in England, nurse?" asked Lady Mary.

"No, my lady, not now; but I remember my father told me that this animal once existed in numbers in different countries of Europe; he said they were still to be found in Norway, Sweden, Russia, Germany, and even in France.* The beaver abounds mostly in North America, and in its cold portions; in solitudes that no foot of man but the wild Indian has ever penetrated—in lonely streams and inland lakes—these harmless creatures are found fulfilling God's purpose, and doing injury to none.

"I think if there had been any beavers in the land of Israel in Solomon's time, that the wise king who spake of ants, spiders, grasshoppers, and conies,† would have named the beavers also, as patterns of

---

* The remains of beaver dams in Wales prove that this interesting animal was once a native of Great Britain.

† The rock rabbits of Judæa.

gentleness, cleanliness, and industry. They work together in bands, and live in families, and never fight or disagree. They have no chief or leader; they seem to have neither king nor ruler; yet they work in perfect love and harmony. How pleasant it would be, Lady Mary, if all Christian people would love each other as these poor beavers seem to do."

"Nurse, how can beavers cut down trees; they have neither axes nor saws?"

"Here, Lady Mary, are the axes and saws with which God has provided these little creatures;" and Mrs. Frazer showed Lady Mary two long curved tusks, of a reddish-brown colour, which she told her were the tools used by the beavers to cut and gnaw the trees; she said she had seen trees as thick as a man's leg that had been felled by these simple tools.

Lady Mary was much surprised that such small animals could cut through anything so thick.

"In nature," replied her nurse, "we often see great things done by very small means. Patience and perseverance work well. The poplar, birch, and some other trees, on which beavers feed, and which they also use in making their dams, are softer and more easily cut than oak, elm, or birch would be: these trees are found growing near the water, and in such places as the beavers build in. The settler owes to the industrious habits of this animal those large open tracts of land called beaver meadows, covered with long, thick, rank grass, which he cuts down and uses as hay. These beaver meadows have the appearance of dried-up lakes. The soil is black and spongy; for you may put a stick down to the depth of many feet. It is only in the months of July, August, and September, that they are dry. Bushes of black alder, with a few poplars and twining shrubs, are scattered over the beaver meadows, some of which have high stony banks, and little islands of trees. On these are many pretty wildflowers; among others, I found growing on the dry banks some real hare-bells, both blue and white."

"Ah, dear nurse, hare-bells! did you find real hare-bells, such as grow on the bonny Highland hills among the heather? I wish papa would let me go to the Upper Province to see the beaver meadows, and gather the dear blue-bells."

"My father, Lady Mary, wept when I brought him a handful of these flowers; for he said it reminded him of his Highland home. I have found these pretty bells growing on the wild hills about Rice Lake, near the water, as well as near the beaver meadows."

"Do the beavers sleep in the winter time, nurse?"

"They do not lie torpid, as racoons do, though they may sleep a good deal; but as they lay up a great store of provisions for the winter, of course they must awake sometimes to eat it."

Lady Mary thought so too.

"In the spring, when the long warm days return, they quit their winter retreat, and separate in pairs, living in holes in the banks of lakes and rivers, and do not unite again till the approach of the cold calls them together to prepare for winter, as I told you."

"Who calls them all to build their winter houses?" asked the child.

"The providence of God, usually called instinct, that guides these animals; doubtless it is the law of nature given to them by God.

"There is a great resemblance in the habits of the musk-rat and the beaver. They all live in the water; all separate in the spring, and meet again in the fall to build and work together; and, having helped each other in these things, they retire to a private dwelling, each family to its own. The otter does not make a dam, like the beaver, and I am not sure that, like the beaver, it works in companies: it lives on fish and roots; the musk-rat on shell-fish and roots; and the beaver on vegetable food mostly. Musk-rats and beavers are used for food, but the flesh of the otter is too fishy to be eaten."

"Nurse, can people eat musk-rats?" asked Lady Mary, with surprise.

"Yes, my lady; in the spring months the hunters and Indians reckon them good food. I have eaten them myself, but I did not like them; they were too fat. Musk-rats build a little house of rushes, and plaster it; they have two chambers, and do not lie torpid; they build in shallow, rushy places in lakes, but in spring they quit their winter houses and are often found in holes among the roots of trees. They live on mussels and shell-fish. The fur is used in making caps, and hats, and fur gloves."

"Nurse, did you ever see a tame beaver?"

"Yes, my dear; I knew a squaw who had a tame beaver, which she used to take out in her canoe with her, and it sat in her lap, or on her shoulder, and was very playful." Just then the dinner-bell rang, and as dinner at Government House waits for no one, Lady Mary was obliged to defer hearing more about beavers until another time.

CHAPTER VIII.

INDIAN BOY AND HIS PETS—TAME BEAVER AT HOME—KITTEN, WILDFIRE—PET RACOON AND THE SPANIEL PUPPIES—CANADIAN FLORA.

"NURSE, you have told me a great many nice stories; now I can tell you one, if you would like to hear it;" and the Governor's little daughter fixed her bright eyes, beaming with intelligence, on the face of her nurse, who smiled, and said she should like very much to hear the story.

"You must guess what it is to be about, nurse."

"I am afraid I shall not guess right. Is it 'Little Red Riding Hood,' or 'Old Mother Hubbard,' or 'Jack the Giant-killer?'"

"Oh, nurse, to guess such silly stories!" said the little girl, stopping her ears. "Those are too silly for me even to tell baby! My story is a nice story about a darling tame beaver. Major Pickford took me on his knee and told me the story last night."

Mrs. Frazer begged Lady Mary's pardon for making such foolish guesses, and declared she should like very much to hear Major Pickford's story of the tame beaver.

"Well, nurse, you must know there was once a gentleman who lived in the bush, on the banks of a small lake, somewhere in Canada, a long, long way from Montreal. He lived all alone in a little log-house, and spent his time in fishing and trapping and hunting; and he was very dull, for he had no wife, and no little child like me to talk to. The only people whom he used to see were some French lumberers; and now and then the Indians would come in their canoes and fish on his lake, and make their wigwams on the lake-shore, and hunt deer in the wood. The gentleman was very fond of the Indians, and used to pass a great deal of his time with them, and talk to them in their own language.

"Well, nurse, one day he found a poor little Indian boy who had been lost in the woods, and was half starved, sick, and weak; and the kind gentleman took him home to his house, and fed and nursed him till he got quite strong again. Was not that good, nurse?"

"It was quite right, my lady. People should always be kind to the sick and weak, and especially to a poor Indian stranger. I like the story very much, and shall be glad to hear more about the Indian boy."

"Nurse, there is not a great deal more about the Indian boy; for when the Indian party to which he belonged returned from hunting, he went away to his own home; but I forgot to tell you that the gentleman had often said how much he should like to have a young beaver to make a pet of. He was very fond of pets; he had a dear little squirrel, just like mine, nurse, a flying squirrel, which he had made so tame that it slept in his bosom and lived in his pocket, where he kept nuts and acorns and apples for it to eat; and he had a racoon too, nurse—only think, a real racoon! and Major Pickford told me something so droll about the racoon, only I want first to go on with the story about the beaver.

"One day, as the gentleman was sitting by the fire reading, he heard a slight noise, and when he looked up was quite surprised to see an Indian boy in a blanket coat, with his dark eyes fixed upon his face, while his long black hair hung down on his shoulders. He looked quite wild, and did not say a word, but only opened his blanket coat, and showed a brown-furred animal asleep on his breast. What do you think it was, nurse?"

"A young beaver, my lady."

"Yes, nurse, it was a little beaver. The good Indian boy had caught it and tamed it on purpose to bring it to his white friend, who had been so good to him.

"I cannot tell you all the amusing things the Indian boy said about the beaver, though the Major told them to me; but I cannot talk like an Indian, you know, Mrs. Frazer. After the boy went away, the gentleman set to work and made a little log-house for his beaver to live in, and set it in a corner of the shanty; and he hollowed a large sugar-trough for its water, that it might have water to wash in; and cut down some young willows and poplars and birch-trees for it to eat. And the little beaver grew very fond of its new master; it would fondle him just like a little squirrel, put its soft head on his knee, and climb up on his lap. He taught it to eat bread, sweet cake, and biscuit, and even roast and boiled meat; and it would drink milk too.

"Well, nurse, the little beaver lived very happily with this kind gentleman till the next fall, and then it began to get very restless and active, as if it were tired of doing nothing. One day its master heard of the arrival of a friend some miles off, so he left the beaver to take care of itself, and went away; but he did not forget to give it some green wood, and plenty of water to drink and play in. He stayed several days, for he was very glad to meet with a friend in that lonely place; but when he came back, he could not open his door, and was obliged to get in at the window. What do you think the beaver had done? It had built a dam against the side of the trough, and a wall across the door; and it had dug up the hearth and the floor, and carried the earth and the stones to help to make its dam, and puddled it with water, and made such work! The house was in perfect confusion, with mud, chips, bark, and stone; and oh, nurse, worse than all that, it had gnawed through the legs of the table and chairs, and they were lying on the floor in such a state; and it cost the poor gentleman so much trouble to put things to rights again, and make more chairs and another table! and when I laughed at the pranks of that wicked beaver—for I could not help laughing—the Major pinched my ear, and called me a mischievous puss."

Mrs. Frazer was very much entertained with the story, and she told Lady Mary that she had heard of tame beavers doing such things before; for in the season of the year when beavers congregate together to repair their works and build their winter houses, those that are in confinement become restless and unquiet, and show the instinct that moves these animals to provide their winter retreats, and lay up their stores of food.

"Nurse," said Lady Mary, "I did not think that beavers and racoons could be taught to eat sweet cake, and bread, and meat."

"Many animals learn to eat very different food to what they are accustomed to live upon in a wild state. The wild cat lives on raw flesh; while the domestic cat, you know, my dear, will eat cooked meat, and even salt meat, with bread and milk and many other things. I knew a person who had a black kitten called 'Wildfire,' which would sip whisky toddy out of his glass, and seemed to like it as well as milk or water, only it made him too wild and frisky."

"Nurse, the racoon that the gentleman had would drink sweet whisky punch; but my governess said it was not right to give it to him; and Major Pickford laughed, and declared the racoon must have looked very funny when he was tipsy. Was not the Major naughty to say so?"

Mrs. Frazer said it was not quite proper.

"But, nurse, I have not told you about the racoon. He was a funny fellow. He was very fond of a little spaniel and her puppies, and took a great deal of care of them. He brought them meat, and anything nice that had been given him to eat; but one day he thought he would give them a fine treat, so he contrived to catch a poor cat by the tail, and drag her into his den, where he and the puppies lived together. His pets, of course, would not eat the cat, so the wicked creature ate up poor pussy himself; and the gentleman was so angry with the naughty thing that he killed him and made a cap of his skin, for he was afraid the cunning racoon would kill his beaver and eat up his tame squirrel."

"The racoon, Lady Mary, in its natural state, has all the wildness and cunning of the fox and weasel. He will eat flesh, poultry, and sucking pigs, and is also very destructive to Indian corn. These creatures abound in the Western States, and are killed in great numbers for their skins. The Indian hunters eat the flesh, and say it is very tender and good; but it is not used for food in Canada. The racoon belongs to the same class of animals as the bear, which it resembles in some points, though, being small, it is not so dangerous either to man or the larger animals.

" And now, my dear, let me show you some pretty wild-flowers a little girl brought me this morning for you, as she heard that you loved flowers. There are yellow-mocassins, or ladies'-slippers, the same that I told you of a little while ago; and white lilies, crane-bills, and these pretty lilac geraniums; here are scarlet cups, and blue lupines—they are all in bloom now—and many others. If we were on the Rice Lake Plains, my lady, we could gather all these, and many, many more. In the months of June and July those plains are like a garden, and their roses scent the air."

" Nurse, I will ask my dear papa to take me to the Rice Lake Plains," said the little girl, as she gazed with delight on the lovely Canadian flowers.

CHAPTER IX.

NURSE TELLS LADY MARY ABOUT A LITTLE BOY WHO WAS EATEN BY A BEAR IN THE PROVINCE OF NEW BRUNSWICK— OF A BABY THAT WAS CARRIED AWAY, BUT TAKEN ALIVE —A WALK IN THE GARDEN—HUMMING-BIRDS—CANADIAN BALSAMS.

"NURSE," said Lady Mary, "did you ever hear of any one having been eaten by a wolf or bear?"

"I have heard of such things happening, my dear, in this country; but only in lonely, unsettled parts, near swamps and deep woods."

"Did you ever hear of any little boy or girl having been carried off by a wolf or bear?" asked the child.

"No, my lady, not in Canada, though similar accidents may have happened there; but when I was a young girl I heard of such tragedies at New Brunswick—one of the British provinces lying to the east of this, and a cold and rather barren country, but containing many minerals, such as coal, limestone, and marble, besides vast forests of pine, and small lakes and rivers. It resembles Lower Canada in many respects; but it is not so pleasant as the province of Upper Canada, neither is it so productive.

"Thirty years ago it was not so well cleared or cultivated as it is now, and the woods were full of wild beasts that dwelt among the swamps and wild rocky valleys. Bears, and wolves, and catamounts abounded, with foxes of several kinds, and many of the fine-furred and smaller species of animals, which were much sought for on account of their skins. Well, my dear, near the little village where my aunt and uncle were living, there were great tracts of unbroken swamps and forests, which of course sheltered many wild animals. A sad accident happened a few days before we arrived, which caused much sorrow and no little fright in the place.

"An old man went out into the woods one morning with his little grandson to look for the oxen, which had strayed from the clearing. They had not gone many yards from the enclosure when they heard a crackling and rustling among the underwood and dry timber that strewed the ground. The old man, thinking it was caused by the cattle they were looking for, bade the little boy go forward and drive them on the track; but in a few minutes he heard a fearful cry from the child, and hurrying forward through the tangled brushwood, saw the poor little boy in the deadly grasp of a huge black bear, which was making off at a fast trot with his prey.

"The old man was unarmed, and too feeble to pursue the dreadful beast. He could only wring his hands and rend his gray hairs in grief and terror; but his lamentations could not restore the child to life. A band of hunters and lumberers, armed with rifles and knives, turned out to beat the woods, and were not long in tracking the savage animal to his retreat in a neighbouring cedar swamp. A few fragments of the child's dress were all that remained of him; but the villagers had the satisfaction of killing the great she-bear with her two half-grown cubs. The magistrates of the district gave them a large sum for shooting these creatures, and the skins were sold, and the money given to the parents of the little boy; but no money could console them for the loss of their beloved child.

"The flesh of the bear is eaten both by Indians and hunters; it is like coarse beef. The hams are cured and dried, and by many thought to be a great dainty."

"Mrs. Frazer, I would not eat a bit of the ham made from a wicked, cruel bear, that eats little children," said Lady Mary. "I wonder the hunters were not afraid to go into the swamps where such savage beasts lived. Are there as many bears and wolves now in those places?"

"No, my lady; great changes have taken place since that time. As the country becomes more thickly settled, the woods disappear. The axe and the fire destroy the haunts that sheltered these wild beasts, and they retreat further back, where the deer and other creatures on which they principally feed abound."

"Do the hunters follow them?"

"There is no place, however difficult or perilous, where the hunter will not venture in search of game."

"And do they pursue the graceful deer? They are so pretty, with their branching antlers and slender limbs, that I should have thought no man could be so cruel as to slay them."

"But their flesh is very savoury, and the Indian, when tired of bear's meat, is glad of a dish of fresh venison. So with his gun—if he has one—or with his bow and arrow, he lies in wait among the foliage and brushwood of the forest, or behind the rocks on the bank of some swift torrent, and when the unsuspecting stag makes his appearance on the opposite crag, he takes a careful aim, lets fly his rapid arrow, and seldom fails to kill his victim; which, dropping into the stream below, is borne by the current within his reach."

"They are brave men, those hunters," said Lady Mary; "but I fear they are very cruel. I wish they would only kill the furious bears. That was a sad story you told me just now, nurse, about the poor little boy. Have you heard of any other sufferers; or do people sometimes escape from these monsters?"

"I also heard of a little child," continued nurse, "not more than two years old, who was with her mother in the harvest-field, who had spread a shawl on the ground near a tall tree, and laid the child upon it to sleep or play, when a bear came out of

HUNTING THE DEER.

THE BEAR AND THE BABY.

THE HARVEST-FIELD.

the wood and carried her off, leaping the fence with her in his arms. But the mother ran screaming after the beast, and the reapers pursued so closely with their pitch-forks and reaping-hooks, that Bruin, who was only a half-grown bear, being hard pressed, made for a tree; and as it was not easy to climb with a babe in his arms, he quietly laid the little one down at the foot of the tree, and soon was among the thick branches out of the reach of the enemy. I daresay baby must have wondered what rough nurse had taken her up; but she was unhurt, and is alive now."

"I am so glad, nurse, the dear baby was not hugged to death by that horrid black bear; and I hope he was killed."

"I daresay, my lady, he was shot by some of the men; for they seldom worked near the forest without having a gun with them, in case of seeing deer, or pigeons, or partridges."

"I should not like to live in that country, Mrs. Frazer; for a bear, a wolf, or a catamount might eat me."

"I never heard of a governor's daughter being eaten by a bear," said Mrs. Frazer, laughing, as she noticed the earnest expression on the face of her little charge. She then continued her account of the ursine family.

"The bear retires in cold weather, and sleeps till warmer seasons awaken him. He does not lay up any store of winter provisions, because he seldom rouses himself during the time of his long sleep; and in the spring he finds food, both vegetable and animal, for he can eat anything when hungry, like the hog. He often robs the wild bees of their honey, and his hide, being so very thick, seems insensible to the stings of the angry bees. Bruin will sometimes find odd places for his winter bed, for a farmer, who was taking a stack of wheat into his barn to be threshed in the winter time, once found a large black bear comfortably asleep in the middle of the sheaves."

"How could the bear have got into the stack of wheat, nurse?"

"The claws of this animal are so strong, and he makes so much use of his paws, which are almost like hands, that he must have pulled the sheaves out and so made an entrance for himself. His skin and flesh amply repaid the farmer for any injury the grain had received. I remember seeing the bear brought home in triumph on the top of the load of wheat. Bears often do great mischief by eating the Indian corn when it is ripening; for besides what they devour, they spoil a vast deal by trampling the plants down with their clumsy feet. They will, when hard pressed by hunger, come close to the farmer's house and rob the pig-sty of its tenants. Many years ago, before the forest was cleared away in the neighbourhood of what is now a large town, but in those days consisted of only a few poor log-houses, a settler was much annoyed by the frequent visits of a bear to his hog-pen. At last he resolved to get a neighbour who was a very expert hunter to come with his rifle and watch with him. The pen where the fatling hogs were was close to the log-house; it had a long, low, shingled roof, and was carefully fastened up, so that no bear could find entrance. Well, the farmer's son and the hunter had watched for two nights, and no bear came; on the third they were both tired, and lay down to sleep upon the floor of the kitchen, when the farmer's son was awakened by a sound as of some one tearing and stripping the

"CAUGHT AT LAST."

shingles from the pen. He looked out; it was moonlight, and there he saw the dark shadow of some tall figure on the ground, and spied the great black bear standing on its hinder legs, and pulling the shingles off as fast as it could lay its big black paws upon them. The hogs were in a great fright, screaming and grunting with terror. The young man stepped back into the house, roused up the hunter, who took aim from the doorway, and shot the bear dead. The head of the huge beast was nailed up as a trophy, and the meat was dried or salted for winter use, and great were the rejoicings of the settlers, who had suffered so much from Bruin's thefts of corn and pork."

"I am glad the hunter killed him, nurse; for he might have eaten up some of the little children, when they were playing about in the fields."

"Sometimes," continued Mrs. Frazer, "the bears used to visit the sugar-bush, when the settlers were making maple sugar, and overturn the sap-troughs, and drink the sweet liquid. I daresay they would have been glad of a taste of the sugar too, if they could have got at it. The bear is not so often met with now as it used to be many years ago. The fur of the bear used to be worn as muffs and tippets, but is now little used for that purpose, being thought to be too coarse and heavy; but it is still made into caps for soldiers, and used for sleigh-robes."

This was all Mrs. Frazer chose to recollect about bears, for she was unwilling to dwell long on any gloomy subject, which she knew was not good for young minds: so she took her charge into the garden to look at the flower-beds, and watch the birds and butterflies; and soon the child was gaily running from flower to flower, watching with childish interest the insects flitting to and fro. At last she stopped, and holding up her finger to warn Mrs. Frazer not to come too near, stood gazing in wonder and admiration on a fluttering object that was hovering over the full-blown honey-suckles on a trellis near the greenhouse. Mrs. Frazer approached her with due caution.

"Nurse," whispered the child, "look at that curious moth with a long bill like a bird; see its beautiful shining colours. It has a red necklace, like mamma's rubies. Oh, what a curious creature! It must be a moth or a butterfly. What is it?"

"It is neither a moth nor a butterfly, my dear. It is a humming-bird."

"Oh, nurse, a humming-bird—a real humming-bird!—pretty creature! But it is gone. Oh, nurse, it darts through the air as swift as an arrow! What was it doing—looking at the honey-suckles? I daresay it thought them very pretty; or was it smelling them? They are very sweet."

"My dear child, he might be doing so; I don't know. Perhaps the good God has given to these creatures the same senses for enjoying sweet scents and bright colours as we have; yet it was not for the perfume, but the honey, that this little bird came to visit the open flowers. The long slender bill, which the humming-bird inserts into the tubes of the flowers, is his instrument for extracting the honey. Look at the pretty creature's ruby throat, and green and gold feathers."

"How does it make that whirring noise, nurse, just like the humming of a top?" asked the child.

"The little bird produces the sound, from which he derives his name, by beating the air with his wings. This rapid motion is necessary to sustain his position in the air while sucking the flowers.

"I remember, Lady Mary, first seeing humming-birds when I was about your age, while walking in the garden. It was a bright September morning, and the rail-fences and every dry twig of the brushwood were filled with the webs of the field-spider. Some, like thick white muslin, lay upon the grass; while others were suspended from trees like forest lace-work, on the threads of which the dewdrops hung like strings of shining pearls; and hovering round the flowers were several ruby-throated humming-birds, the whirring of whose wings as they beat the air sounded like the humming of a spinning-wheel. And I thought, as I gazed upon them, and the beautiful lace webs that hung among the bushes, that they must have been the work of these curious creatures, which had made them to catch flies, and had strung the bright dewdrops thereon to entice them—so little did I know of the nature of these birds. But my father told me a great deal about them, and read me some very pretty things about humming-birds; and one day, Lady Mary, I will show you a stuffed one a friend gave me, with its tiny nest and eggs not bigger than peas."

Lady Mary was much delighted at the idea of seeing the little nest and eggs, and Mrs. Frazer said, "There is a wild-flower* that is known to the Canadians by the name of the Humming-flower, on account of the fondness which those birds evince for it. This plant grows on the moist banks of creeks. It is very beautiful, of a bright orange-scarlet colour. The stalks and stem of the plant are almost transparent. Some call it Speckled Jewels, for the bright blossoms are spotted with dark purple; and some, Touch-me-not."

"That is a droll name, nurse," said Lady Mary. "Does it prick one's finger like a thistle?"

"No, my lady; but when the seed-pods are nearly ripe, if you touch them they spring open and curl into little rings, and the seed drops out."

"Nurse, when you see any of these curious flowers, will you show them to me?"

Mrs. Frazer said they would soon be in bloom, and promised Lady Mary to bring her some, and to show her the singular manner in which the pods burst. "But, my lady," said she, "the gardener will show you the same thing in the greenhouse. As soon as the seed-pods of the balsams in the pots begin to harden they will spring and curl, if touched,

---

* *Noli me tangere*, Canadian Balsam.

and drop the seeds like the wild plant; for they belong to the same family. But it is time for your ladyship to go in."

When Lady Mary returned to the schoolroom, her governess read to her some interesting accounts of the habits of the humming-bird.

"'This lively little feathered gem—for in its hues it unites the brightness of the emerald, the richness of the ruby, and the lustre of the topaz—includes in its wide range more than one hundred species. It is the smallest, and at the same time the most brilliant, of all the American birds. Its headquarters may be said to be among the glowing flowers and luxurious fruits of the torrid zone and the tropics. But one species, the ruby-throated, is widely diffused, and is a summer visitor all over North America, even within the arctic circle, where, for a brief space of time, it revels in the ardent heat of the short-lived summer of the north. Like the cuckoo, it follows the summer wherever it flies.

"'The ruby-throated humming-bird * is the only species that is known in Canada. With us it builds and breeds, and then returns to summer skies and warmer airs. The length of the humming-bird is only three inches and a half, and four and a quarter in extent from one tip of the wing to the other. When on the wing the bird has the form of a cross, the wings forming no curve, though the tail is depressed during the time that it is poised in the act

* *Trochilus rubus.*

of sucking the honey of the flower. The tongue is long and slender; the bill long and straight; the legs are very short, so that the feet are hardly visible when on the wing. They are seldom seen walking, but rest on the slender sprigs when tired. The flight is so rapid that it seems without effort. The humming sound is produced by the wing, in the act of keeping itself balanced while feeding in this position. They resemble the hawk-moth, which also keeps up a constant vibratory motion with its wings. This little creature is of a temper as fierce and fiery as its plumes, often attacking birds of treble its size; but it seems very little disturbed by the near approach of the human species, often entering open windows, and hovering around the flowers in the flower-stand; it has even been known to approach the vase on the table, and insert its bill among the flowers, quite fearless of those persons who sat in the room. Sometimes these beautiful creatures have suffered themselves to be captured by the hand.

" 'The nest of the ruby-throated humming-bird is usually built on a mossy branch. At first sight it looks like a tuft of gray lichens, but when closely examined shows both care and skill in its construction, the outer wall being of fine bluish lichens cemented together, and the interior lined with the silken threads of the milk-weed, the velvety down of the tall mullein, or the brown hair-like filaments of the fern. These, or similar soft materials, form the bed of the tiny young ones. The eggs are white, two in number, and about the size of a pea, but oblong in shape. The parents hatch their eggs in about ten days, and in a week the little ones are able to fly, though the old birds continue to supply them with honey for some time longer. The Mexican Indians give the name of Sunbeam to the humming-bird, either in reference to its bright plumage or its love of sunshine.

" 'The young of the humming-bird does not attain its gay plumage till the second year. The male displays the finer colours—the ruby necklace being confined to the old male bird. The green and coppery lustre of the feathers is also finer in the male bird.' "

Lady Mary was much pleased with what she had heard about the humming-bird, and she liked the name of Sunbeam for this lovely creature.

CHAPTER X.

AURORA BOREALIS, OR NORTHERN LIGHTS, MOST FREQUENTLY SEEN IN NORTHERN CLIMATES—CALLED MERRY DANCERS—ROSE TINTS—TINT-LIKE APPEARANCE—LADY MARY FRIGHTENED.

ONE evening, just as Mrs. Frazer was preparing to undress Lady Mary, Miss Campbell, her governess, came into the nursery, and taking the little girl by the hand, led her to the window, and bade her look out on the sky towards the north, where a low dark arch, surmounted by an irregular border, like a silver fringe, was visible. For some moments Lady Mary stood silently regarding this singular appearance; at length she said, "It is a rainbow, Miss Campbell; but where is the sun that you told me shone into the drops of rain to make the pretty colours?"

"It is not a rainbow, my dear; the sun has been long set."

"Can the moon make rainbows at night?" asked the little girl.

"The moon does sometimes, but very rarely, make what is called a *lunar* rainbow. Luna was the

THE AURORA BOREALIS.

ancient name for the moon. But the arch you now see is caused neither by the light of the sun nor of the moon, but is known by the name of Aurora Borealis, or Northern Lights. The word Aurora means morning or dawn; and Borealis, northern. You know, my dear, what is meant by the word dawn; it is the light that is seen in the sky before the sun rises."

Lady Mary replied, "Yes, Miss Campbell, I have often seen the sun rise, and once very early too, when I was ill, and could not sleep; for nurse lifted me in her arms out of bed, and took me to the window. The sky was all over of a bright golden colour, with streaks of rosy red; and nurse said, 'It is dawn; the sun will soon be up.' And I saw the beautiful sun rise from behind the trees and hills. He came up so gloriously, larger than when we see him in the middle of the sky; and I could look at him without hurting my eyes."

"Sunrise is indeed a glorious sight, my dear; but He who made the sun is more glorious still. Do you remember what we read yesterday in the Psalms?—

"Verse 1. The heavens declare the glory of God: and the firmament sheweth His handywork.
2. One day telleth another: and one night certifieth another.
3. There is neither speech nor language: but their voices are heard among them.
5. In them hath He set a tabernacle for the sun: which cometh forth as a bridegroom out of his chamber, and rejoiceth as a giant to run his course.

"The Northern Lights, Lady Mary, are frequently visible in Canada, but are most brilliant in the colder regions near the North Pole, where they serve to give light during the dark season to those dismal countries from which the sun is so many months absent. The light of the Aurora Borealis is so soft and beautiful, that any object can be distinctly seen; though in those cold countries there are few human beings to be benefited by this beautiful provision of Nature."

"The wild beasts and birds must be glad of the pretty lights," said the child thoughtfully; for Lady Mary's young heart always rejoiced when she thought that God's gifts could be shared by the beasts of the field and the fowls of the air, as well as by mankind.

"Look now, my dear," said Miss Campbell, directing the attention of her pupil to the horizon; "what a change has taken place whilst we have been speaking! See, the arch is sending up long shafts of light; now they divide, and shift from side to side, gliding along among the darker portions of vapour like moving pillars."

"Ah, there, there they go!" cried the little girl, clapping her hands with delight. "See, nurse, how the pretty lights chase each other and dance about! Up they go, higher and higher! How pretty they look! But now they are gone! They are fading away. I am so sorry," said the child, despondingly, for a sudden cessation had taken place in the motions of the heavens.

"We will go in for a little time, my dear," said her governess, "and then look out again. Great changes take place sometimes in these aërial phenomena in a few minutes."

"I suppose," said Lady Mary, "these lights are the same that the peasants of Northern England and Ireland call the Merry Dancers?"

"Yes, they are the same; and they fancy that they are seen when war and troubles are about to break out. But this idea is a very ignorant one; for were that the case, some of the cold countries of the world, where the sky is illumined night after night by the Aurora Borealis, would be one continual scene of misery. I have seen in this country a succession of these lights for four or five successive nights. This phenomenon owes its origin to *electricity*, which is a very wonderful agent in nature, and exists in various bodies, perhaps in all created things. It is this that shoots across the sky in the form of lightning, and causes the thunder to be heard; circulates in the air we breathe; occasions whirlwinds, waterspouts, earthquakes, and volcanoes, and makes one substance attract another.

"Look at this piece of amber. If I rub it on the table, it will become warm to the touch. Now I will take a bit of thread and hold near it. See, the thread moves towards the amber and clings to it. Sealing-wax and many other substances when heated have this property. Some bodies give out flashes and sparks by being rubbed. If you stroke a black cat briskly in the dark, you will see faint flashes of light come from her fur; and on very cold nights in the winter season, flannels that are worn next the skin crackle and give sparks when taken off and shaken."

These things astonished Lady Mary. She tried the experiment with the amber and thread, and was much amused by seeing the thread attracted; and she wanted to see the sparks from the cat's back, only there happened, unfortunately, to be no black cat or kitten in Government House. Mrs. Frazer, however, promised to procure a beautiful black kitten for her, that she might enjoy the singular sight of the electric sparks from its coat; and Lady Mary wished winter were come, that she might see the sparks from her flannel petticoat and hear the sounds.

"Let us now go and look out again at the sky," said Miss Campbell; and Lady Mary skipped joyfully through the French window to the balcony, but ran back, and flinging her arms about her nurse, cried out, in accents of alarm, "Nurse, nurse, the sky is all closing together! Oh, Miss Campbell, what shall we do?"

"There is no cause for fear, my dear child; do not be frightened. There is nothing to harm us."

Indeed, during the short time they had been absent, a great and remarkable change had taken place in the appearance of the sky. The electric fluid had diffused itself over the face of the whole heavens; the pale colour of the streamers had changed to bright rose, pale violet, and greenish-yellow. At the zenith, or that part more immediately overhead, a vast ring of deep indigo was presented to the eye; from this swept down, as it were, a flowing curtain of rosy light, which wavered and moved incessantly, as if agitated by a gentle breeze, though a perfect stillness reigned through the air. The child's young heart was awed by this sublime spectacle; it seemed to her as if it were indeed the throne of the great Creator of the world that she was gazing upon; and she veiled her face in her nurse's arms and trembled exceedingly, even as the children of Israel when the fire of Mount Sinai was revealed, and they feared to behold the glory of the Most High God. After a while, Lady Mary, encouraged by the cheerful voices of her governess and nurse, ventured to look up to watch the silver stars shining dimly as from beneath a veil, and she whispered to herself the words that her governess had before repeated to her: "The heavens declare the glory of God, and the firmament sheweth his handywork."

After a little while, Mrs. Frazer thought it better to put Lady Mary to bed, as she had been up much longer than usual, and Miss Campbell was afraid lest the excitement should make her ill; but the child did not soon fall asleep, for her thoughts were full of the strange and glorious things she had seen that night.

CHAPTER XI.

STRAWBERRIES—CANADIAN WILD FRUITS—WILD RASP-
BERRIES—THE HUNTER AND THE LOST CHILD—CRAN-
BERRIES—CRANBERRY MARSHES—NUTS.

ONE day Lady Mary's nurse brought her a small Indian basket, filled with ripe red strawberries.

"Nurse, where did you get these nice strawberries?" said the little girl, peeping beneath the fresh leaves with which they were covered.

"I bought them from a little Indian squaw in the street; she had brought them from a wooded meadow some miles off, my lady. They are very fine; see, they are as large as those that the gardener sent in yesterday from the forcing-house; and these wild ones have grown without any pains having been bestowed upon them."

"I did not think, nurse, that wild strawberries could have been so fine as these; may I taste them?"

Mrs. Frazer said she might. "These are not so large, so red, or so sweet as some that I have gathered when I lived at home with my father," said the nurse. "I have seen acres and acres of strawberries, as large as the early scarlet that are sold so high in the market, on the Rice Lake plains. When the farmers have ploughed a fallow on the Rice Lake plains, the following summer it will be covered with a crop of the finest strawberries. I have gathered pailsful day after day; these, however, have been partly cultivated by the plough breaking up the sod; but they seem as if sown by the hand of Nature. These fruits and many sorts of flowers appear on the new soil that were never seen there before. After a fallow has been chopped, logged, and burned, if it be left for a few years, trees, shrubs, and plants, will cover it, unlike those that grew there before."

"That is curious," said the child. "Does God sow the seeds in the new ground?"

"My lady, no doubt they come from Him, for He openeth His hand, and filleth all things living with plenteousness. My father, who thought a great deal on these subjects, said that the seeds of many plants may fall upon the earth, and yet none of them take root till the soil be favourable for their growth. It may be that these seeds had lain for years, preserved in the earth till the forest was cleared away, and the sun, air, and rain caused them to spring up; or the earth may still bring forth the herb of the field, after its kind, as in the day of the creation; but whether it be so or not, we must bless the Lord for His goodness and for the blessings that He giveth us at all times."

THE WILD GOOSEBERRY.

"Are there many sorts of wild fruits fit to eat, nurse, in this country? Please, will you tell me all that you know about them?"

"There are so many, Lady Mary, that I am afraid I shall weary you before I have told you half of them."

"Nurse, I shall not be tired, for I like to hear about fruits and flowers very much; and my dear mamma likes you to tell me all you know about the plants, trees, birds, and beasts of Canada."

"Besides many sorts of strawberries, there are wild currants, both black and red, and many kinds of wild gooseberries," said Mrs. Frazer. "Some grow on wastes by the roadside, in dry soil, others in swamps; but most gooseberries are covered with thorns, which grow not only on the wood, but on the berries themselves."

"I would not eat those disagreeable, thorny gooseberries; they would prick my tongue," said the little girl.

"They cannot be eaten without first being scalded. The settlers' wives contrive to make good pies and preserves with them, by first scalding the fruit and then rubbing it between coarse linen cloths. I have heard these tarts called thornberry pies, which, I think, was a good name for them. When emigrants first come to Canada and clear the backwoods, they have little time to make nice fruit-gardens for themselves, and they are glad to gather the wild berries that grow in the woods and swamps to make tarts and preserves; so that they do not even despise the thorny gooseberries or the wild black currants. Some swamp-gooseberries, however, are quite smooth, of a dark red colour, but small, and they are very nice when ripe. The blossoms of the wild currants are very beautiful, of a pale yellowish-green, and hang down in long graceful branches; the fruit is harsh, but makes wholesome preserves. But there are thorny currants as well as thorny gooseberries; these have long, weak, trailing branches; the berries are small, covered with stiff bristles, and of a pale red colour. They are not wholesome; I have seen people made very ill by eating them; I have heard even of their dying in consequence of having done so."

"I am sure, nurse, I will not eat those wild currants," said Lady Mary; "I am glad you have told me about their being poisonous."

"This sort is not often met with, my dear; and these berries, though they are not good for man, doubtless give nourishment to some of the wild creatures that seek their food from God, and we have enough dainties and to spare without them.

"The red raspberry is one of the most common and the most useful to us of the wild fruits. It grows in abundance all over the country—by the roadside, in the half-opened woods, on upturned roots, or in old neglected clearings; there is no place so wild but it will grow, wherever its roots can find a crevice. With maple sugar, the farmers' wives never need lack a tart nor a dish of fruit and cream.

The poor Irish emigrants' children go out and gather pailsful, which they carry to the towns and villages to sell. The birds, too, live upon the fruit, and flying away with it to distant places, help to sow the seed. A great many small animals eat the ripe raspberry, for even the racoon and great black bear come in for their share."

"The black bears! O nurse! O Mrs. Frazer!" exclaimed Lady Mary, in great astonishment. "What! do bears eat raspberries?"

"Yes, indeed, my lady, they do. Bears are fond of all ripe fruits. The bear resembles the hog in all its tastes very closely; both in their wild state will eat flesh, grain, fruit, and roots.

"There is a story about a bear and an Indian hunter, which will show how bears eat berries. It is from the Journal of Peter Jacobs, the Indian missionary:—

"'At sunrise, next morning,' he says, 'we tried to land, but the water was so full of shoals, we could not without wading a great distance.

"'The beach before us was of bright sand, and the sun was about, when I saw an object moving on the shore: it appeared to be a man, and seemed to be making signals of distress. We were all weary and hungry, but thinking it was a fellow-creature in distress, we pulled towards him. Judge of our surprise when the stranger proved to be an enormous bear!

"'He was seated on his hams, and what we thought his signals, were his raising himself on his hind legs to pull down the berries from a high bush, and with his paws full, sitting down again to eat them at his leisure.

"'Thus he continued daintily enjoying his ripe fruit in the posture some lapdogs are taught to assume while eating. On we pulled, and forgot our hunger and weariness: the bear still continued breakfasting.

"'We got as close on shore as the shoals would permit, and John (one of the Indians), taking my double-barrelled gun, leaped into the water, gun in hand, and gained the beach. Some dead brushwood hid the bear from John's sight, but from the canoe we could see both John and the bear.

"'The bear now discovered us, and advanced towards us; and John, not seeing him for the bush, ran along the beach towards him. The weariness from pulling all night, and having eaten no food, made me lose my presence of mind; for I now remembered that the gun was only loaded with duck-shot, and you might as well meet a bear with a gun loaded with pease.

"'John was in danger, and we strained at our paddles to get to his assistance; but as the bear was a very large one, and as we had no other firearms, we should have been but poor helps to John in the hug of a wounded bear. The bear was at the other side of the brush-heap; John heard the dry branches cracking, and he dodged into a hollow under a bush. The bear passed, and was coursing along the sand, but as he passed by where John lay, bang went the gun. The bear was struck.

"'We saw him leap through the smoke to the very spot where we had last seen John. We held our breath; but instead of the cry of agony we expected to hear from John, bang went the gun again—John is not yet caught. Our canoe rushed through the water—we might yet be in time; but my paddle fell from my hand with joy, as I saw John pop his head above the bush, and with a shout point to the side of the log on which he stood, 'There he lies, dead enough.' We were thankful indeed to our Great Preserver.'

"Though fruit and vegetables seem to be the natural food of the bear, they also devour flesh, and even fish—a fact of which the good Indian missionary assures us, and which I shall tell you, Lady Mary, in his own words:—

"'A few evenings after we left the *Rock*, while the men were before me 'tracking' (towing the canoe), by pulling her along by a rope from the shore, I observed behind a rock in the river what I took to be a black fox. I stole upon it as quietly as possible, hoping to get a shot; but the animal saw me, and waded to the shore. It turned out to be a young bear fishing. The bear is a great fisherman. His mode of fishing is very curious. He wades into a current, and seating himself upright on his hams, lets the water come about up to his shoulders; he patiently waits until the little fishes come along and rub themselves against his sides; he seizes them instantly, gives them a nip, and with his left paw tosses them over his shoulder to the shore. His left paw is always the one used for tossing ashore the produce of his fishing. Feeling is the sense of which Bruin makes use here, not sight.

"'The Indians of that part say that the bear catches sturgeon when spawning in the shoal-water, but the only fish that I know of their catching is the sucker. Of these, in the months of April and May, the bear makes his daily breakfast and supper, devouring about thirty or forty at a meal. As soon as he has caught a sufficient number, he wades ashore and regales himself on the best morsels, which are the thick of the neck, behind the gills. The Indians often shoot him when thus engaged.'

"There is a small red berry in the woods that is known by the name of the bear-berry,* of which they say the young bears are particularly fond."

"I should be afraid of going to gather raspberries, nurse, for fear of the bears coming to eat them too."

"The hunters know that the bears are partial to this fruit, and often seek them in large thickets where they grow. A young gentleman, Lady Mary, once went out shooting game, in the province of New Brunswick, in the month of July, when the weather was warm, and there were plenty of wild berries ripe. He had been out for many hours, and at last found himself on the banks of a creek. But the

---

* *Arbutus uva ursi.*—"Kinnikinnick" is the Indian name.

bridge he had been used to cross was gone, having been swept away by heavy rains in the spring. Passing on a little higher up, he saw an old clearing full of bushes, and knowing that wild animals were often to be met with in such spots, he determined to cross over and try his luck for a bear, a racoon, or a young fawn. Not far from the spot he saw a large fallen swamp elm-tree, which made a capital bridge. Just as he was preparing to cross, he heard the sound of footsteps on the dry crackling sticks, and saw a movement among the raspberry bushes. His finger was on the lock of his rifle in an instant, for he thought it must be a bear or a deer; but just as he was about to fire, he saw a small, thin, brown hand, all red and stained from the juice of the ripe berries, reaching down a branch of the fruit. His very heart leaped within him with fright, for in another moment he would have shot the poor little child that, with wan, wasted face, was looking at him from between the raspberry bushes. It was a little girl, about as old as you are, Lady Mary. She was without hat or shoes, and her clothes were all in tatters. Her hands and neck were quite brown and sun-burned. She seemed frightened at first, and would have hid herself, had not the stranger called out gently to her to stay, and not to be afraid; and then he hurried over the log bridge, and asked her who she was, and where she lived. And she said 'she did not live anywhere, for she was lost.' She could not tell how many days, but she thought she had been seven nights out in the woods. She had been sent to take some dinner to her father, who was at work in the forest, but had missed the path, and gone on a cattle track, and did not find her mistake until it was too late, when she became frightened, and tried to get back, but only lost herself deeper in the woods. The first night she wrapped her frock about her head, and lay down beneath the shelter of a great upturned root. She had eaten but little of the food she had in the basket that day, for it lasted her nearly two. After it was gone she chewed some leaves, till she came to the raspberry clearing, and got berries of several kinds, and plenty of water to drink from the creek. One night, she said, she was awakened by a heavy tramping near her, and looking up in the moonlight, saw two great black beasts, which she thought were her father's oxen; and so she sat up and called, 'Buck,' 'Bright,'—for these were their names; but they had no bells, and looked like two great shaggy black dogs. They stood on their hind legs upright and looked at her, but went away. These animals were bears, but the child did not know that; and she said she felt no fear, for she said her prayers every night before she lay down to sleep, and she knew that God would take care of her, both sleeping and waking."

"And did the hunter take her home?" asked Lady Mary, who was much interested in the story.

"Yes, my dear, he did. Finding that the poor little girl was very weak, the young man took her on

THE LOST CHILD AND THE BEARS.

his back. Fortunately he happened to have a little wine in a flask, and a bit of dry biscuit in his knapsack, and this greatly revived the little creature.

Sometimes she ran by his side, while holding by his coat, talking to her new friend, seemingly quite happy and cheerful, bidding him not be afraid even if they had to pass another night in the wood; but just as the sun was setting, they came out of the dark forest into an open clearing.

"It was not the child's home, but a farm belonging to a miller who knew her father, and had been in search of her for several days; and he and his wife were very glad when they saw the lost child, and gladly showed her preserver the way. They rejoiced very much when the poor wanderer was restored safe and well to her sorrowing parents."

"Nurse," said Lady Mary, "I am so glad the good hunter found the little girl. I must tell my own dear mamma that nice story. How sorry my mamma and papa would be to lose me in the woods!"

The nurse smiled, and said, "My dear lady, there is no fear of such an accident happening to you. You are not exposed to the same trials and dangers as the children of poor emigrants; therefore you must be very grateful to God, and do all you can to serve and please Him; and when you are able, be kind and good to those who are not so well off as you are."

"Are there any other wild fruits, nurse, besides raspberries and strawberries, and currants and gooseberries?"

"Yes, my dear lady, a great many more. We

will begin with wild plums: these we often preserve; and when the trees are planted in gardens, and taken care of, the fruit is very good to eat. The wild cherries are not very nice; but the bark of the black cherry is good for agues and low fevers. The choke cherry is very beautiful to look at, but hurts the throat, closing it up if many are eaten, and making it quite sore. The huckle-berry is a sweet, dark blue berry, that grows on a very delicate low shrub: the blossoms are very pretty, pale pink or greenish white bells: the fruit is very wholesome; it grows on light dry ground, on those parts of the country that are called plains in Canada. The settlers' children go out in parties, and gather great quantities, either to eat or dry for winter use. These berries are a great blessing to every one, besides forming abundant food for the broods of young quails and partridges; squirrels, too, of every kind eat them. There are blackberries also, Lady Mary; and some people call them thimble-berries."

"Nurse, I have heard mamma talk about black-berries."

"The Canadian blackberries are not so sweet, I am told, my lady, as those at home, though they are very rich and nice-tasted; neither do they grow so high. Then there are high-bush cranberries, and low-bush cranberries. The first grow on a tall bush, and the fruit has a fine appearance, hanging in large bunches of light scarlet among the dark green leaves; but they are very, very sour, and take a great deal of sugar to sweeten them. The low-bush cranberries grow on a slender, trailing plant; the blossom is very pretty, and the fruit about the size of a common gooseberry, of a dark purplish red, very smooth and shining; the seeds are minute, and lie in the white pulp within the skin: this berry is not nice till it is cooked with sugar. There is a large cranberry marsh somewhere at the back of Kingston, where vast quantities grow. I heard a young gentleman say that he passed over this tract when he was hunting, while the snow was on the ground, and that the red juice of the dropped berries dyed the snow crimson beneath his feet. The Indians go every year to a small lake called Buckhorn Lake, many miles up the river Otonabee, in the Upper Province, to gather cranberries; which they sell to the settlers in the towns and villages, or trade away for pork, flour, and clothes. The cranberries, when spread out on a dry floor, will keep fresh and good for a long time. Great quantities of cranberries are brought to England from Russia, Norway, and Lapland, in barrels, or large earthen jars, filled with spring water; but the fruit thus roughly preserved must be drained, and washed many times, and stirred with sugar, before it can be put into tarts, or it would be salt and bitter. I will boil some cranberries with sugar, that you may taste them; for they are very wholesome."

Lady Mary said she should like to have some in her own garden.

"The cranberry requires a particular kind of soil, not usually found in gardens, my dear lady; for as the cranberry marshes are often covered with water in the spring, I suppose they need a damp, cool soil, near lakes or rivers; perhaps sand, too, may be good for them. But we can plant some berries, and water them well; in a light soil they may grow, and bear fruit, but I am not sure that they will do so. Besides these fruits, there are many others, that are little used by man, but are of great service as food to the birds and small animals. There are many kinds of nuts, too—filberts, with rough prickly husks, walnuts, butternuts, and hickory-nuts; these last are large trees, the nuts of which are very nice to eat, and the wood very fine for cabinet-work, and for fire-wood: the bark is used for dyeing. Now, my dear, I think you must be quite tired with hearing so much about Canadian fruits."

Lady Mary said she was glad to learn that there were so many good things in Canada, for she heard a lady say to her mamma that it was an ugly country, with nothing good or pretty in it.

"There is something good and pretty to be found everywhere, my dear child, if people will but open their eyes to see it, and their hearts to enjoy the good things that God has so mercifully spread abroad for us and all his creatures to enjoy. But Canada is really a fine country, and is fast becoming a great one."

CHAPTER XII.

GARTER-SNAKES—RATTLE-SNAKES—ANECDOTE OF A LITTLE BOY—FISHERMAN AND SNAKE—SNAKE CHARMERS—SPIDERS—LAND-TORTOISE.

"NURSE, I have been so terrified. I was walking in the meadow, and a great snake—so big, I am sure"—and Lady Mary held out her arms as wide as she could—"came out of a tuft of grass. His tongue was like a scarlet thread, and had two sharp points; and, do you know, he raised his wicked head, and hissed at me. I was so frightened that I ran away. I think, Mrs. Frazer, it must have been a rattle-snake. Only feel now how my heart beats"—and the little girl took her nurse's hand, and laid it on her heart.

"What colour was it, my dear?" asked her nurse.

"It was green and black, chequered all over; and it was very large, and opened its mouth very wide, and showed its red tongue. It would have killed me, if it had bitten me, would it not, nurse?"

"It would not have harmed you, my lady; or even if it had bitten you, it would not have killed you. The chequered green snake of Canada is not poisonous. It was more afraid of you than you were of it, I make no doubt."

"Do you think it was a rattle-snake, nurse?"

"No, my dear; there are no snakes of that kind in Lower Canada, and very few below Toronto. The winters are too cold for them. But there are plenty in the western part of the Province, where the summers are warmer, and the winters milder. The rattle-snake is a dangerous reptile, and its bite causes death, unless the wound be burned or cut out. The Indians apply different sorts of herbs to the wound. They have several plants, known by the names of rattle-snake root, rattle-snake weed, and snake root. It is a good thing that the rattlesnake gives warning of its approach before it strikes the traveller with its deadly fangs. Some people think that the rattle is a sign of fear, and that it would not wound people if it were not afraid they were coming near to hurt it. I will tell you a story, Lady Mary, about a brave little boy. He went out nutting one day with another boy about his own age; and while they were in the grove gathering nuts, a large black snake, that was in a low tree, dropped down and suddenly coiled itself round the throat of his companion. The child's screams were dreadful; his eyes were starting from his head with pain and terror. The other, regardless of the danger, opened a clasp-knife that he had in his pocket, and seizing the snake near the head, cut it apart, and so saved his friend's life, who was well-nigh strangled by the tight folds of the rep-

A BOY-HERO.

tile, which was one of a very venomous species, the bite of which generally proves fatal."

"What a brave little fellow!" said Lady Mary. "You do not think it was cruel, nurse, to kill the snake?" she added, looking up in Mrs. Frazer's face.

"No, Lady Mary, for he did it to save a fellow-creature from a painful death; and we are taught by God's Word that the soul of man is precious in the sight of his Creator. We should be cruel were we wantonly to inflict pain upon the least of God's creatures; but to kill them in self-defence, or for necessary food, is not cruel: for when God made Adam, He gave him dominion, or power, over the beasts of the field, and the fowls of the air, and every creeping thing. It was an act of great courage and humanity in the little boy, who perilled his own life to save that of his helpless comrade, especially as he was not naturally a child of much courage, and was very much afraid of snakes: but love for his friend entirely overcame all thoughts of his own personal danger.*

"The large garter-snake which you saw, my dear lady, is comparatively harmless. It lives on toads and frogs, and robs the nests of young birds, and also pilfers the eggs. Its long forked tongue enables it to catch insects of different kinds; it will even eat fish, and for that purpose frequents the water as well as the black snake.

"I heard a gentleman once relate a circumstance

---

* A fact related to me by a gentleman from the State of Vermont, as an instance of impulsive feeling overcoming natural timidity.

to my father that surprised me a good deal. He was fishing one day in a river near his own house, but, being tired, he seated himself on a log or fallen tree, where his basket of fish also stood; when a large garter-snake came up the log, and took a small fish out of his basket, which it speedily swallowed. The gentleman, seeing the snake so bold as not to mind his presence, took a small rock-bass by the tail, and half in joke held it towards it, when, to his great surprise, the snake glided towards him, took the fish out of his hand, and sliding away with its prize to a hole beneath the log, began by slow degrees to swallow it, stretching its mouth and the skin of its neck to a very great extent; till, after a long while, it was fairly gorged, and then it slid down its hole, leaving its head and neck only to be seen."

"I should have been so frightened, nurse, if I had been the gentleman, when the snake came to take the fish," said Lady Mary.

"The gentleman was well aware of the nature of the reptile, and knew that it would not bite him. I have read of snakes of the most poisonous kinds being tamed and taught all manner of tricks. There are in India and Egypt people that are called snake-charmers, who contrive to extract the fangs containing the venom from the Cobra da capella, or hooded snake; which then become quite harmless. These snakes are very fond of music, and will come out of the leather bag or basket that their master carries them in, and will dance or run up his arms, twining about his neck, and even entering his mouth! They do not tell people that the poison-teeth have been extracted, so that it is thought to be the music that keeps the snake from biting. The snake has a power of charming birds and small animals, by fixing its eye steadily upon them, when the little creatures become paralyzed with fear, either standing quite still, or coming nearer and nearer to their cruel enemy, till they are within his reach. The cat has the same power, and can by this art draw birds from the tops of trees within her reach. These little creatures seem unable to resist the temptation of approaching her, and, even when driven away, will return from a distance to the same spot, seeking, instead of shunning, the danger which is certain to prove fatal to them in the end. Some writers assert that all wild animals have this power in the eye, especially those of the cat tribe, as the lion and tiger, leopard and panther. Before they spring upon their prey, the eye is always steadily fixed, the back lowered, the neck stretched out, and the tail waved from side to side; if the eye is averted, they lose the animal, and do not make the spring."

"Are there any other kinds of snakes in Canada, nurse," asked Lady Mary, "besides the garter-snake?"

"Yes, my lady, several; the black snake, which is the most deadly, next to the rattle-snake, is sometimes called the puff-adder, as it inflates the skin of the head and neck when angry. The copper-bellied snake is also poisonous. There is a small snake of a deep grass-green colour sometimes seen in the fields and open copse-woods. I do not think it is dangerous; I never heard of its biting any one. The stareworm is also harmless. I am not sure whether the black snakes that live in the water are the same as the puff or black adder. It is a great blessing, my dear, that these deadly snakes are so rare, and do so little harm to man. Indeed I believe they would never harm him, were they let alone; but if trodden upon, they cannot know that it was by accident, and so put forth the weapons that God has armed them with in self-defence. The Indians in the north-west, I have been told, eat snakes, after cutting off their heads. The cat also eats snakes, leaving the head; she will also catch and eat frogs—a thing I have witnessed myself, and know to be true.* One day a snake fixed itself on a little girl's arm, and wound itself around it. The mother of the child was too much terrified to tear the deadly creature off, but filled the air with cries. Just then a cat came out of the house, and quick as lightning sprang upon the snake, and fastened on its neck; which caused the reptile to uncoil its folds, and it fell to the earth in the grasp of the cat. Thus the child's life was saved, and the snake killed. Thus you see, my dear, that God provided a preserver for this little one when no

---

* I once saw a half-grown kitten eat a live green frog, which she first brought into the parlour, playing with it as with a mouse.

help was nigh. Perhaps the child cried to Him for aid, and He heard her and saved her by means of the cat."

Lady Mary was much interested in all that Mrs. Frazer had told her. She remembered having heard some one say that the snake would swallow her own young ones, and she asked her nurse if it was true, and if they laid eggs.

"The snake will swallow her young ones," said Mrs. Frazer. "I have seen the garter-snake open her mouth and let the little ones run into it when danger was nigh. The snake also lays eggs: I have seen and handled them often. They are not covered with a hard, brittle shell, like that of a hen, but with a sort of whitish skin, like leather: they are about the size of a blackbird's egg, long in shape; some are rounder and larger. They are laid in some warm place, where the heat of the sun and earth hatches them. But though the mother does not brood over them, as a hen does over her eggs, she seems to take great care of her little ones, and defends them from their many enemies by hiding them out of sight in the singular manner I have just told you. This love of offspring, my dear child, has been wisely given to all mothers, from the human mother down to the very lowest of the insect tribe. The fiercest beast of prey loves its young, and provides food and shelter for them; forgetting its savage nature to play with and caress them. Even the spider, which is a disagreeable insect, fierce and unloving to its fellows, displays the tenderest care for its brood, providing a safe retreat for them in the fine silken cradle she spins to envelop the eggs, which she leaves in some warm spot, where she secures them from danger: some glue a leaf down, and overlap it, to insure it from being agitated by the winds, or discovered by birds. There is a curious spider, commonly known as the nursing spider, which carries her sack of eggs with her wherever she goes; and when the young ones come out, they cluster on her back, and so travel with her; when a little older, they attach themselves to the old one by threads, and run after her in a train."

Lady Mary laughed, and said she should like to see the funny little spiders all tied to their mother, trotting along behind her.

"If you go into the meadow, my dear," said Mrs. Frazer, "you will see on the larger stones some pretty shining little cases, quite round, looking like gray satin."

"Nurse, I know what they are," said Lady Mary. "Last year I was playing in the green meadow, and I found a piece of granite with several of these satin cases. I called them silk pies, for they looked like tiny mince pies. I tried to pick one off, but it stuck so hard that I could not, so I asked the gardener to lend me his knife; and when I raised the crust it had a little rim under the top, and I slipped the knife in, and what do you think I saw? The pie was full of tiny black shining spiders; and they ran out, such a number of them,—more than I could count, they ran so fast. I was sorry I opened the crust, for it was a cold, cold day, and the little spiders must have been frozen, out of their warm air-tight house."

"They are able to bear a great deal of cold, Lady Mary—all insects can; and even when frozen hard, so that they will break if any one tries to bend them, yet when spring comes again to warm them, they revive, and are as full of life as ever. Caterpillars thus frozen will become butterflies in due time. Spiders, and many other creatures, lie torpid during the winter, and then revive in the same way as dormice, bears, and marmots do."

"Nurse, please will you tell me something about tortoises and porcupines?" said Lady Mary.

"I cannot tell you a great deal about the tortoise, my dear," replied her nurse. "I have seen them sometimes on the shores of the lakes, and once or twice I have met with the small land-tortoise, in the woods on the banks of the Otonabee river. The shell that covers these reptiles is black and yellow, divided into squares—those which I saw were about the size of my two hands. They are very harmless creatures, living chiefly on roots and bitter herbs: perhaps they eat insects as well. They lie buried in the sand during the long winters, in a torpid state: they lay a number of eggs, about the size of a blackbird's, the shell of which is tough and soft, like a snake's egg. The old tortoise buries these in the loose sand near the water's edge, and leaves them to be hatched by the heat of the sun. The little tortoise, when it comes out of the shell, is about as big as a large spider—it is a funny-looking thing. I have heard some of the Indians say that they dive into the water, and swim, as soon as they are hatched; but this I am not sure of. I saw one about the size of a crown-piece that was caught in a hole in the sand: it was very lively, and ran along the table, making a rattling noise with its hard shell as it moved. An old one that one of my brothers brought in he put under a large heavy box, meaning to feed and keep it; but in the morning it was gone: it had lifted the edge of the box and was away, nor could he find out how it had contrived to make its escape from the room. This is all that I know about the Canadian land-tortoise."

CHAPTER XIII.

ELLEN AND HER PET FAWNS—DOCILITY OF FAN—JACK'S DROLL TRICKS—AFFECTIONATE WOLF—FALL FLOWERS—DEPARTURE OF LADY MARY—THE END.

ONE day Lady Mary came to seek her nurse in great haste, and describe to her a fine deer that had been sent as a present to her father by one of his Canadian friends. She said the great antlers were to be put up over the library door.

"Papa called me down to see the poor dead deer, nurse; and I was very sorry it had been killed: it was such a fine creature. Major Pickford laughed when I said so; but he promised to get me a live fawn. Nurse, what is a fawn?"

"It is a young deer, my lady."

"Nurse, please can you tell me anything about fawns? Are they pretty creatures, and can they be tamed; or are they fierce, wild little things?"

"They are very gentle animals; and, if taken young, can be brought up by sucking the finger like a young calf or a pet lamb. They are playful and lively, and will follow the person who feeds them, like a dog. They are very pretty, of a pale dun or red colour, with small white spots on the back like large hailstones; the eyes are large, and soft, and black, with a very meek expression in them; the hoofs are black and sharp: they are clean and delicate in their habits, and easy and graceful in their movements.

"I remember," continued Mrs. Frazer, "to have heard of a sad accident which was caused by a fawn."

"Oh, what was it, nurse? Do tell me, for I don't see how such a timid pretty creature could hurt any one."

"A party of Indians were rowing in a canoe on one of the great American rivers. As they passed a thick clump of trees, a young fawn suddenly sprang out, and, frightened by their cries, leaped into the water. For some days the rain had been heavy; the river was therefore running with a wild, impetuous current; and the fawn was carried along by the rushing tide at a tremendous rate. The Indians, determined to capture it, paddled down the stream with eager haste, and in their excitement forgot that they were in the neighbourhood of a great rapid, or cataract; dangerous at all times, but especially so after long-continued rains. On, on, they went! Suddenly the fawn disappeared, and looking behind them, the startled Indians found themselves on the very brink of the rapid! Two of their countrymen, standing on a rock overhanging the foaming waters,

A PERILOUS SITUATION. 191

GOING DOWN THE RAPIDS.

saw their peril, and by shouts and gestures warned them of it. With vigorous efforts they turned the prow of their canoe, and endeavoured to cross the river. They plied their paddles with all the desperation of men who knew that nothing could save them but their own exertions, that none on earth could help them. But the current proved too strong. It carried them over the fall, and dashed their bark broadside against a projecting rock. A moment, and all was over! Not one of them was ever seen again!"

"Oh, what a sad story!" cried Lady Mary; "and all those men were killed through one poor little fawn! Still, nurse, it was not the fawn's fault; it was the result of their own impatience and folly. Did you ever see a tame fawn, nurse?"

"I have seen many, my dear, and I can tell you of one that was the pet and companion of a little girl whom I knew several years ago. A hunter had shot a poor doe, which was very wrong, and contrary to the Indian hunting law; for the native hunter will not, unless pressed by hunger, kill the deer in the spring of the year, when the fawns are young. The Indian wanted to find the little one after he had shot the dam, so he sounded a decoy whistle, to imitate the call of the doe; and the harmless thing answered it with a bleat, thinking no doubt it was its mother calling to it. This betrayed its hiding-place, and it was taken unhurt by the hunter, who took it home, and gave it to my little friend Ellen to feed and take care of."

"Please, Mrs. Frazer, will you tell me what sort of trees hemlocks are? Hemlocks in England are poisonous weeds."

THE INDIAN HUNTER. 193

THE INDIAN HUNTER.

"These are not weeds, but large forest trees—a species of pine. I will show you some the next time we go out for a drive—they are very handsome trees."

"And what are creeks, nurse?"

"Creeks are small streams, such as in Scotland would be termed 'burns,' and in England 'rivulets.'"

"Now, nurse, you may go on about the dear little fawn; I want you to tell me all you know about it."

"Little Ellen took the poor timid thing, and laid it in an old Indian basket near the hearth, and put some wool in it, and covered it with an old cloak to keep it warm; and she tended it very carefully, letting it suck her fingers dipped in warm milk, as she had seen the dairy-maid do in weaning young calves. In a few days it began to grow strong and lively, and would jump out of its basket, and run bleating after its foster-mother: if it missed her from the room, it would wait at the door watching for her return.

"When it was older, it used to run on the grass plot in the garden: but if it heard its little mistress's step or voice in the parlour, it would bound through the open window to her side; and her call of 'Fan, Fan, Fan,' would bring it home from the fields near the edge of the forest. But poor Fan got killed by a careless boy throwing some fire-wood down upon it, as it lay asleep in the wood-shed. Ellen's grief was very great, but all she could do was to bury it in the garden near the river-side, and plant lilac bushes around its little green-sodded grave."

"I am so sorry, nurse, that this good little girl lost her pretty pet."

"Some time after the death of 'Fan,' Ellen had another fawn given to her. She called this one Jack,—it was older, larger, and stronger, but was more mischievous and frolicsome than her first pet. It would lie in front of the fire on the hearth, like a dog, and rub its soft velvet nose against the hand that patted it very affectionately, but gave a good deal of trouble in the house: it would eat the carrots, potatoes, and cabbages, while the cook was preparing them for dinner; and when the housemaid had laid the cloth for dinner, Jack would go round the table and eat up the bread she had laid to each plate, to the great delight of the children, who thought it good fun to see him do so.

"Ellen put a red leather collar about Jack's neck, and some months after this he swam across the rapid river, and went off to the wild woods, and was shot by some hunters, a great many miles away from his old home, being known by his fine red collar. After the sad end of her two favourites, Ellen would have no more fawns brought in for her to tame."

Lady Mary was much interested in the account of the little girl and her pets. "Is this all you know about fawns, nurse?"

"I once went to call on a clergyman's wife who lived in a small log-house near a new village. The youngest child, a fat baby of two years old, was lying on the rug before a large log-fire, fast asleep;

its little head was pillowed on the back of a tame half-grown fawn that lay stretched on its side, enjoying the warmth of the fire, as tame and familiar as a spaniel dog. This fawn had been brought up with the children, and they were very fond of it, and would share their bread and milk with it at meal times; but it got into disgrace by gnawing the bark of the young orchard-trees, and cropping the bushes in the garden; besides, it had a trick of opening the cupboard, and eating the bread, and drinking any milk it could find. So the master of the house gave it away to a baker who lived in the village; but it did not forget its old friends, and used to watch for the children going to school, and as soon as it caught sight of them, it would trot after them, poking its nose into the basket to get a share of their dinner, and very often managed to get it all!"

"And what became of this nice fellow, nurse?"

"Unfortunately, my lady, it was chased by some dogs, and ran away to the woods near the town, and never came back again. Dogs will always hunt tame fawns when they can get near them; so it seems a pity to domesticate them only to be killed in so cruel a way. The forest is the best home for these pretty creatures, though even there they have many enemies besides the hunter. The bear, the wolf, and the wolverine kill them. Their only means of defence lies in their fleetness of foot. The stag will defend himself with his strong horns; but the doe and her little fawn have no such weapons to guard themselves when attacked by beasts of prey. The wolf is one of the greatest enemies they have."

"I hate wolves," said Lady Mary; "wolves can never be tamed, nurse."

"I have heard and read of wolves being tamed, and becoming very fond of their masters. A gentleman in Canada once brought up a wolf puppy, which became so fond of him that when he left it to go home to England, it, refused to eat, and died of grief at his absence! Kindness will tame even fierce beasts, who soon learn to love the hand that feeds them. Bears and foxes have often been kept tame in this country, and eagles and owls; but I think they cannot be so happy shut up, away from their natural companions and habits, as if they were free to go and come at their own will."

"I should not like to be shut up, nurse, far away from my own dear home," said the little girl, thoughtfully. "I think, sometimes, I ought not to keep my dear squirrel in a cage—shall I let him go?"

"My dear, he has now been so used to the cage, and to have all his daily wants supplied, that I am sure he would suffer from cold and hunger at this season of the year if he were left to provide for himself; and if he remained here the cats and weasels might kill him."

"I will keep him safe from harm, then, till the warm weather comes again; and then, nurse, we will take him to the mountain, and let him go, if he likes to be free, among the trees and bushes."

It was now the middle of October; the rainy season that usually comes in the end of September and beginning of October in Canada was over. The soft, hazy season, called Indian summer, was come again; the few forest leaves that yet lingered were ready to fall—bright and beautiful they still looked, but Lady Mary missed the flowers.

"I do not love the fall—I see no flowers now, except those in the greenhouse. The cold, cold winter, will soon be here again," she added sadly.

"Last year, dear lady, you said you loved the white snow, and the sleighing, and the merry bells, and wished that winter would last all the year round."

"Ah, yes, nurse; but I did not know how many pretty birds and flowers I should see in the spring and the summer; and now they are all gone, and I shall see them no more for a long time."

"There are still a few flowers, Lady Mary, to be found; look at these."

"Ah, dear nurse, where did you get them? How lovely they are!"

"Your little French maid picked them for you, on the side of the mountain. Rosette loves the wild-flowers of her native land."

"Nurse, do you know the names of these pretty starry flowers on this little branch, that look so light and pretty?"

"These are asters; a word, your governess told me the other day, meaning star-like. Some people call these flowers Michaelmas daisies. These lovely lilac asters grow in light, dry ground; they are among the prettiest of our fall flowers. These with the small white starry flowers crowded upon the stalks, with the crimson and gold in the middle, are dwarf asters."

"I like these white ones, nurse; the little branches look so nicely loaded with blossoms; see, they are quite bowed down with the weight of all these flowers."

"These small shrubby asters grow on dry gravelly banks of lakes and rivers."

"But here are some large dark purple ones."

"These are also asters. They are to be found on dry wastes, in stony, barren fields, and by the corners of rail-fences; they form large spreading bushes, and look very lovely, covered with their large dark purple flowers. There is no waste so wild, my lady, but the hand of the Most High can plant it with some blossom, and make the waste and desert place flourish like a garden. Here are others, still brighter and larger, with yellow disks, and sky-blue flowers. These grow by still waters, near mill-dams and swampy places. Though they are larger and gayer, I do not think they will please you so well as the small ones that I first showed you; they do not fade so fast, and that is one good quality they have."

"They are more like the China asters in the garden, nurse, only more upright and stiff; but here is another sweet blue flower—can you tell me its name?"

"No, my dear; you must ask your governess."

Lady Mary carried the nosegay to Miss Campbell, who told her the blue flower was called the Fringed Gentian, and that the gentians and asters bloomed the latest of all the autumn flowers in Canada. Among these wild-flowers, she also showed her the large dark blue bell-flowered gentian, which was indeed the last flower of the year.

"Are there no more flowers in bloom now, nurse?" asked the child, as she watched Mrs. Frazer arranging them for her in a flower-glass.

"I do not know of any now in bloom but the Golden Rods and the latest of the Everlastings. Rosette shall go out and try to get some of them for you. The French children make little mats and garlands of them to ornament their houses, and to hang on the little crosses above the graves of their friends, because they do not fade away like other flowers."

Next day, Rosette, the little nursery-maid, brought Lady Mary an Indian basket full of Sweet-scented Everlastings. This flower had a fragrant smell; the leaves were less downy than some of the earlier sorts, but were covered with a resinous gum that caused it to stick to the fingers; it looked quite silky, from the thistle-down, which, falling upon the leaves, was gummed down to the surface.

"'The country folks," said Mrs. Frazer, "call this plant Neglected Everlasting, because it grows on dry wastes by road-sides, among thistles and fire-weed; but I love it for its sweetness; it is like a true friend

—it never changes. See, my dear, how shining its straw-coloured blossoms and buds are, just like satin flowers."

"Nurse, it shall be my own flower," said the little girl; "and I will make a pretty garland of it, to hang over my own dear mamma's picture. Rosette says she will show me how to tie the flowers together; she has made me a pretty wreath for my doll's straw hat, and she means to make her a mat and a carpet too."

The little maid promised to bring her young lady some wreaths of the festoon pine—a low creeping plant, with dry, green, chaffy leaves, that grows in the barren pine woods, of which the Canadians make Christmas garlands; and also some of the winter berries, and spice berries, which look so gay in the fall and early spring, with berries of brightest scarlet, and shining dark-green leaves, that trail over the ground on the gravelly hills and plains.

Nurse Frazer brought Lady Mary some sweetmeats, flavoured with an extract of the spicy winter-green, from the confectioner's shop; the Canadians being very fond of the flavour of this plant. The Indians chew the leaves, and eat the ripe mealy berries, which have something of the taste of the bay-laurel leaves. The Indian men smoke the leaves as tobacco.

One day, while Mrs. Frazer was at work in the nursery, her little charge came to her in a great state of agitation—her cheeks were flushed, and her eyes were dancing with joy. She threw herself into her arms, and said, "Oh, dear nurse, I am going home to dear old England and Scotland. Papa and mamma are going away from Government House, and I am to return to the old country with them. I am so glad—are not you?"

But the tears gathered in Mrs. Frazer's eyes, and fell fast upon the work she held in her hand. Lady Mary looked surprised, when she saw how her kind nurse was weeping.

"Nurse, you are to go too; mamma says so. Now you need not cry, for you are not going to leave me."

"I cannot go with you, my dearest child," whispered her weeping attendant, "much as I love you; for I have a dear son of my own. I have but him, and it would break my heart to part from him;" and she softly put aside the bright curls from Lady Mary's fair forehead, and tenderly kissed her. "This child is all I have in the world to love me, and when his father, my own kind husband, died, he vowed to take care of me, and cherish me in my old age, and I promised that I would never leave him; so I cannot go away from Canada with you, my lady, though I dearly love you."

"Then, Mrs. Frazer, I shall be sorry to leave Canada; for when I go home, I shall have no one to talk to me about beavers, and squirrels, and Indians, and flowers, and birds."

"Indeed, my lady, you will not want for amusement there, for England and Scotland are finer places than Canada. Your good governess and your new nurse will be able to tell you many things that will delight you;—and you will not quite forget your poor old nurse, I am sure, when you think about the time you have spent in this country."

"Ah, dear good old nurse, I will not forget you," said Lady Mary, springing into her nurse's lap and fondly caressing her, while big bright tears fell from her eyes.

There was so much to do, and so much to think about, before the Governor's departure, that Lady Mary had no time to hear any more stories, nor to ask any more questions about the natural history of Canada; though, doubtless, there were many other curious things that Mrs. Frazer could have related, for she was a person of good education, who had seen and noticed as well as read a great deal. She had not always been a poor woman, but had once been a respectable farmer's wife, though her husband's death had reduced her to a state of servitude; and she had earned money enough while in the Governor's service to educate her son, and this was how she came to be Lady Mary's nurse.

Lady Mary did not forget to have all her Indian curiosities packed up with some dried plants and flower seeds collected by her governess; but she left the cage with her flying squirrel to Mrs. Frazer, to take care of till the following spring, when she told her to take it to the mountain, or St. Helen's Island, and let it go free, that it might be a happy squirrel once more, and bound away among the green trees in the Canadian woods.

When Mrs. Frazer was called in to take leave of the Governor and his lady, after receiving a handsome salary for her care and attendance on their little daughter, the Governor gave her a sealed parchment, which, when she opened, was found to contain a Government deed for a fine lot of land, in a fertile township in Upper Canada.

It was with many tears and blessings that Mrs. Frazer took leave of the good Governor's family; and, above all, of her beloved charge, Lady Mary.

APPENDIX.

The Indians, though so stolid and impassive in their general demeanour, are easily moved to laughter, having a quick perception of fun and drollery, and sometimes show themselves capable of much humour, and even of wit.

The following passage I extract from a Hamilton paper, Canada West, which will, I think, prove amusing to my readers :—

At a missionary meeting in Hamilton, which took place a short time since, John Sunday, a native preacher, was particularly happy in addressing his audience on the objects of the meeting, and towards the close astonished all present by the ingenuity and power of his appeal to their liberality. His closing words are too good to be lost. I give them as they were spoken by him :—

"There is a gentleman who, I suppose, is now in this house. He is a very fine gentleman, but a very modest one. He does not like to show himself at these meetings. I do not know how long it is since I have seen him; he comes out so little. I am very much afraid that he sleeps a great deal of his time when he ought to be out doing good. His name is Gold.—Mr. Gold, are you here to-night, or are you sleeping in your iron chest? Come out, Mr. Gold. Come out and help us to do this great work—to preach the gospel to every creature. Ah, Mr. Gold, you ought to be ashamed of yourself, to sleep so much in your iron chest. Look at your white brother, Mr. Silver. He does a great deal of good while you are sleeping. Come out, Mr. Gold. Look, too, at your little brown brother, Mr. Copper. He is everywhere. Your poor little brown brother is running about doing all he can to help us. Why don't you come out, Mr. Gold? Well, if you won't show yourself, send us your *shirt*—that is, a *bank-note!*

"This is all I have to say."

Whether the witty appeal of the Indian had the effect of bringing forth Mr. Gold from his hiding-place is not said, but we hope it moved some of the wealthy among his hearers to contribute a few sovereigns or gold dollars to the missionary work of converting the poor Indians in the far west regions of Canada.

LIST OF INDIAN WORDS.

A-da-min,	The strawberry.
Ah-meek,	The beaver.
Ajidamo,	The red squirrel.
Be-dau-bun,	Dawn of the morning.
Chee-ma-in-in,	Birch canoe.
Chee-to-wàik,	The plover.
Dah-hìnda,	The bull-frog.
Gitche Mànito,	Giver of life. / The Great Spirit.
Ish-koo-dàh,	Fire.
Kah-ga-gèe,	The raven.
Kàw,	No.
Kaw-wìn,	No, no, indeed.
Keen-o-beèk,	Serpent.

Mad-wa-òska,	{ Sound of waves. / Murmur of the waves.
Mun-a-gah,	Blue-berry.
Misko-deèd,	Spring-beauty.
Neè-chee,	Friend.
Nap-a-nee,	Flour.
Nee-me-no-che-shah,	Sweetheart.
Omee-mèe,	The wild pigeon.
Opee-cheé,	The robin.
O-wais-sa,	The blue-bird.
Peta-wan-ooka,	The light of the morning.
Shaw-shaw,	The swallow.
Spook,	Spirit.
Ty-yah!	An exclamation of surprise.
Wai-wassa,	The whip-poor-will.
Wah-ho-no-min,	A cry of lamentation.

Many of the Indian names have been retained in Canada, for various rivers and townships, and are very expressive of the peculiar qualities and features of the country.

www.ingramcontent.com/pod-product-compliance
Lightning Source LLC
Chambersburg PA
CBHW021728220426
43662CB00008B/758